The Sultan's Servants

The Sultan's Servants

THE TRANSFORMATION OF OTTOMAN PROVINCIAL GOVERNMENT, 1550–1650

I. Metin Kunt

Columbia University Press

NEW YORK

1983

THE MODERN MIDDLE EAST SERIES
No. 14
Sponsored by
The Middle East Institute
Columbia University, New York

Library of Congress Cataloging in Publication Data

Kunt, I. Metin, 1942–
    The sultan's servants.

    A revision of the author's thesis (doçent) submitted to the
Inter-University Council in Turkey in 1975 and published in
1978 by Boğaziçi University Press under title: Sancaktan eyalete:
1550–1650 arasinda Osmanlı ümerası ve il idaresi.
    Bibliography: p.
    Includes index.
    1. Local government—Turkey—History. 2. Turkey—
Politics and government—1453–1683. I. Title.
JS6953.A8K86   1983   956.1'01   82-19800
ISBN 0-231-05578-1

Map by Kathleen Borowik, New York City.

Columbia University Press
New York   Guildford, Surrey

Copyright © 1983 Columbia University Press
All rights reserved
Composed by Asco Trade Typesetting Ltd., Hong Kong
Printed in the United States of America

Clothbound editions of Columbia University Press books are
Smyth-sewn and printed on permanent and durable acid-free
paper.

To Kerim

Contents

Figures

Acknowledgments

THIS STUDY IS a prosopographic approach to the analysis of transformations in provincial administration in a crucial period in Ottoman history. The book has a long history of its own. In a sense, insights I gained in three graduate seminars at Princeton provided its foundation: In the spring of 1967 Norman Itzkowitz's seminar on the nineteenth-century Ottoman reform movement concentrated on prosopographic methodology and on the study of Namier, a master of prosopography. That same term Halil İnalcık, then of Ankara, was visiting Princeton and in his seminar, distinguished by his erudition and keen sense of analysis, I had my initiation into the fascinating study of Ottoman documents. The next term David Ayalon of Hebrew University, a leading authority on the late medieval Mamluk state, conducted a seminar on the slave (*mamluk*) institution in Islamic history and on the Mamluk state, where the political-military slave institution had been elevated to its highest level of organization. Professor Ayalon's lectures brought into sharper focus the Islamic background against which Ottoman institutions should be viewed.

As these teachers had considerable influence on my initial efforts to determine the direction and shape of my later research, it gave me added pleasure to return to Princeton to complete the first stage of the project. I spent the academic year 1974–75 at the department of Near Eastern Studies as a visiting fellow where, freed from teaching duties, I was able to study, organize, and analyze the data I had collected in Istanbul from 1971 to 1974. What I worked on in Princeton was a Turkish version, which was submitted to the Inter-University Council in Turkey in September 1975 and defended in April 1976 as a thesis for the *doçent* degree; it was published in 1978 by the Boğaziçi University Press with the title, *Sancaktan Eyalete: 1550–1650 Arasında Osmanlı Ümerası ve İl İdaresi* (From *Sancak* to *Eyalet*: Ottoman Governors and Provincial Administration, 1550–1650). The English version is not just a translation. It is intended for a wider audience including, in addition to Ottoman specialists, historians whose interests lie in other areas or periods, and even non-historians, social scientists perhaps, who might be interested in the transformation of a bureaucracy in a given cultural context and in a certain time period. As such, some sections of the original version have been altered, the discussion of the basic sources has been relegated to appendixes, and all but one of the province lists appended to the Turkish version have been altogether excluded. To make the discussion more meaningful for nonspecialists an introductory chapter has been added and certain other sections, mainly chapters 2, 3, and 5 have been recast and enlarged to present a more general picture.

The preparation of the English version has been delayed partly because I undertook some further research: on the relationship between a governor's official income and his duties (see chapter 2), and on the phenomenon of portions of official revenues being granted continuously, regardless of specific post held (see chapter 5). Also, since the Turkish version was written, I have had to transport my desk no less than three times. I spent the year 1977–78 as a Visiting Associate Professor at Columbia University, and after one term back at Boğaziçi University, I traveled to Jerusalem for an eight-month stay as Fellow of the Institute for Advanced Studies at Hebrew University. The manuscript, started in Istanbul and continued in New York, was finally completed in Jerusalem.

During my years of research in Istanbul I benefited from the comments of Halil İnalcık, now of Chicago, and of the late Cengiz Orhonlu and Mehmed Genç of Istanbul. Many colleagues at Boğaziçi, at Columbia, and at Hebrew University have read and commented on portions of the book. My mentor, Norman Itzkowitz, read both the original version and sections of the English manuscript to suggest improvements in the organization and presentation of the central data. Discussions on the various methodological and substantial aspects of the topic with him, Engin D. Akarlı, and William K. S. Tobin at Princeton made my stay there very pleasant and profitable. At Columbia my hosts T. Halasi-Kun, J. C. Hurewitz, and R. W. Bulliet arranged for a larger group of historians, Ottoman as well as European specialists, to consider aspects of the Ottoman transformation around 1600 at a special conference. I also owe thanks to Gabriel Baer for the very stimulating atmosphere provided at the Institute for Advanced Studies in Jerusalem.

Two recent works on Ottoman institutional history, though they appeared too late to be included in my discussions, should be mentioned here for their relevance. Karl K. Barbir's *Ottoman Rule in Damascus, 1708–1758* (Princeton, 1980), a case study of a particular province at a slightly later date, corroborates my conclusion for the empire as a whole that governors general came to wield significantly increased power. Carter V. Findley's *Bureaucratic Reform in the Ottoman Empire* (Princeton, 1980) is a much broader work on the central bureaucracy in the period of reform (1789–1922); its introductory discussion on earlier functional differentiation of administration will be complemented by the present book.

The original research was supported by a grant from the Boğaziçi University Executive Committee; a further grant from the B. U. Research Center facilitated the additional research. I owe the title to G. E. Aylmer's example, on the excuse that it alliterates in the Ottoman context.

I. Metin Kunt
New York, 1983

Method and Sources

THIS STUDY DEVELOPED as a by-product of my general research on the importance of households in Ottoman polity. In Ottoman historiography there have been studies on the imperial palace—the sultan's household—and on the relationship between the palace and the government. However, not only the sultan but also the leading officials of the empire supported households, made up of their "inner" and "outer" retinues, needed to fulfill their official functions. The make-up of such households, their inter-relations, and their relations with the imperial palace and also with government offices have hitherto been neglected. The political role of Mamluk households, on the other hand, both before and after the Ottoman conquest of Egypt in 1517 have been subjected to quite extensive study.[1] In Ottoman society, too, which shared with the Mamluk state a common theoretical basis and had developed similar institutions, one would expect that both within the ulema (the learned men) who controlled the judicial and educational spheres, and in those groups which participated in military-administrative functions, personal relationships played a major role. Further, one could speculate that various political views and attitudes developed in the context of the households of the leading members of the Ottoman ruling group, and that the interaction between various persons and groups, as well as their relations with the sultan at the top of the imperial order were among the funda-mental features of Ottoman political life.

I then started my research for the purpose of determining the structure and functioning of Ottoman households and ascertaining the validity of the speculations mentioned above. The complexity of the topic forced me to impose some limitations: from the start

my intention was to concentrate the research on members of the
military-administrative elite, the "men of the sword" (*ehl-i seyf*)
as the Ottomans called them. It is true that in Ottoman polity
members of various groups such as the ulema (*ehl-i ilm*, "men of
knowledge"), the "men of the pen" (*ehl-i kalem*)—the bureaucrats,
and the "men of the sword" maintained close personal contacts
with members of other groups; nevertheless, because of the variety
and strength of relationships within each group, it seemed a more
consistent and feasible approach, at least a less cumbersome one, to
study intra-group dynamics.

While thus limiting the subject in content it also seemed
necessary to limit it in time. As the Ottoman political and social
order developed continuously, naturally the polity presented dif-
fering pictures in different periods. I decided to try to determine the
dominant features of the system in two different periods and follow
the change from one to the other in a relatively short time span,
roughly a century, but one in which change had become so perva-
sive and extensive as to deserve to be termed transformation.

The century between 1550 and 1650 was the best suited for
my purposes: Ottoman historians generally agree that the cata-
clysmic events around 1600 and their underlying causes resulted in
a major transformation of government and administration as well
as of Ottoman society in general.[2] The classical institutions of the
Ottoman empire, to use Halil İnalcık's term, emerged during
the reign of Mehmed II, the "conqueror" (of Istanbul, in 1453;
r. 1451–81), and evolved to full maturity in the mid-sixteenth
century. At the end of the century the empire was engaged in
long, costly, and, as it turned out, unprofitable campaigns on two
fronts, against Iran (1578–90) and Austria (1592–1606). Simultaneously, upheavals that started with rural "student" (*suhte*) disturbances and reached a peak during the Celâli revolts proved that
internal order was endangered. Causing a massive dislocation of
Anatolian peasantry, known in Ottoman historiography as the
"great flight" (*büyük kaçgun*), these revolts finally subsided only
after a total mobilization of the forces of the state: the grand vezir
and commander of the imperial forces that succeeded in crushing
and exterminating the rebellious groups was nicknamed "the well-

digger" (*kuyucu*) after his practice of burying in mass graves the multitudes he executed.

Both the various seventeenth-century Ottoman political commentators such as Ayn-i Ali, the unidentified author of *Kitāb-ı Müstetāb*, Koçi Bey, and even Katib Çelebi, although his approach to the problems and his views differ from the earlier writers,[3] and, on the other hand, strong-handed "reformers" such as Murad IV and Köprülü Mehmed Paşa, believed the solution to the problems the empire faced lay in attempting to revive the institutions of the golden age of the mid-sixteenth century.[4] It was only in the eighteenth century that Ottomans came to accept the reality that conditions had vastly changed and that a more radical approach was needed.

There are, of course, different features and aspects of this major transformation. Undoubtedly, in addition to the developments within Ottoman polity itself, the far-reaching advances of the West, which itself underwent a multifaceted political, social, scientific, and cultural transformation in the previous century, had important effects on the Ottoman scene. The exact nature of the various elements contributing to the Ottoman transformation and their relative importance will surely remain a major area of research and debate. My own purpose here is to isolate one single strand within the complex of changes, namely the role of provincial governors, and study it against the background of the general transformation in the period 1550–1650.

While my general research was on Ottoman households, the nature of the data I was able to assemble and the realization that the problem of households was too broad and complex to allow a resolution in the short term forced a third limitation. In addition to restricting my research to the military-administrative groups and to the hundred years from 1550 to 1650, I decided to study only the governors: *sancakbeyi* (district governor) and *beylerbeyi* (governor general), collectively the *ümerā* (commanders), who constitute the most important stratum of the "men of the sword."[5] Again, due to the nature of the major archival sources of this study to be introduced presently, the emphasis was shifted from *ümerā* households to the analysis of the objective conditions of service the governors experienced. Still, the problem of households will remain an important aspect of this analysis, both in relation to the personal origins of the governors and with regard to the economic effects of maintaining households. I hope by taking up only the *ümerā* the purpose of the limitation will be better served; since the purpose was to study a single element of change in terms of its interaction with the other aspects of the general transformation, that is, in terms of how this single element might have been influenced by and how it might have contributed to the general change, it follows that the better defined the single element to be studied the more specific and meaningful the analysis can be.

Prosopography in Ottoman Studies

Not only the dimensions but also the nature of the study is changed with the last limitation mentioned above. Nevertheless, there was no need to abandon the initial methodological approach, that is, basing my attempt to determine the nature of developments in the system on data about persons making up the specific group I am studying. Because of the similarity in approach and method I hope the present study will serve as a foundation for the future stages of my work on households in general.

The basic approach both for the study of households and for the analysis of Ottoman *ümerā* has been the prosopographical method. This method, which can be defined briefly as group biography, has come into increasing use in political-social history in the last thirty or forty years. It is used to study, by means of biographical data, a specific group in terms of, for example, its position in society, its function, its importance, its political or economic power, and its role in social or political change.[6] It has recently come to be applied in Ottoman historiography, though not yet as extensively as in other fields of historical scholarship, and it has already produced some noteworthy results. In the first and still the most important of such new research Norman Itzkowitz studied the personal backgrounds of the members of the various branches of Ottoman administration. By demonstrating that Muslim-born Ottomans also participated in administration and that converts were able to enter the ulema career in the sixteenth century, and further that converts still played an active and significant role in eighteenth-century Ottoman politics, Itzkowitz rejected the then widely accepted model of Ottoman political organization based on the dichotomy of a "ruling institution" versus a "Muslim institution" in terms of function and religious-ethnic background, as well as the view that part of the explanation of Ottoman decline after the seventeenth century was to be found in the "revolt" of the Muslims hitherto excluded from the "ruling institution" to gain entry into the circles of political power. In this study he went on to point out that, at least in the eighteenth century, Ottoman administration was organized along more varied career lines which were primarily functional.[7] More recently Itzkowitz, this time in collaboration with one of his former students, studied the personal backgrounds of *şeyh ül-islām*s, the heads of the ulema hierarchy, just before and during the nineteenth-century Ottoman reform era (*Tanzimat*), to conclude that, at least judged from this group, reform and westernization did not necessarily mean a wholesale renewal of the Ottoman elite.[8]

In other studies on the ulema of earlier periods Soraya Faroqhi described some social conditions affecting this group in the late-sixteenth century, and Ali Uğur attempted a standardized reorganization of a biographical dictionary with a preliminary analysis of the learned profession in the seventeenth century.[9] One final example of prosopographic studies in recent Ottoman historiography, that by Rifaat Ali Abou-el-Haj on high official households, is in fact quite close to my work in terms of groups studied. It seems to me, however, that Abou-el-Haj's attempt is flawed because both the time period he chose to study and the categories of analysis he devised are misleading.[10]

Undoubtedly we owe the accumulation of rich data eminently suitable for prosopographic analysis to certain features of Islamic and Ottoman learned traditions.[11] From the earliest periods of Islam there was a natural curiosity about the personalities in the time of the prophet, a desire to know as much as possible about Muhammad himself and his companions. In time this curiosity turned to scientific interest, both historical and legal. As the traditions and practices of the prophet, his *sunna*, emerged to become a main source, after the Kuran, of the evolving divine law of Islam (*şeriat*), there was a growing need to establish the veracity of the various anecdotes (Hadith) capturing instances of the prophet's actions and utterances. The method devised for this purpose was to check the links in the chains of transmission of these anecdotes; that is, to study the generations and the individuals who related the Hadith to determine when and where they lived, what kind of men they were, what their position on various issues was, in short whether they were trustworthy. The study of history as such and religious-legal studies went in hand; biographical dictionaries became a major output of historians and an indispensible tool for Hadith scholars. Later on, in addition to biographical dictionaries on the successive generations of Muslims, there were compilations for other purposes: the biographies of famous men of a certain city or region, for example, or certain officials of a state were collected.[12]

In the Ottoman cultural context, too, there appeared biographical compilations of all kinds, including specialized collections on various types of officials: among the most famous of such collections are *Davhat ül-Meşāyih* on the *şeyh ül-islām*s, *Hamīlet ül-Küberā* on the chief black eunuchs (*dār üs-saāde ağası*), *Hadīkat ül-Vüzerā* on grand vezirs, and *Sefīnet ül-Rüesā* for heads of the secretariat (*reīs ül-küttāb*). Finally, there appeared in the very last days of the empire the *Sicill-i Osmāni*, the "Ottoman Register," a comprehensive biographical dictionary aiming to include all prominent Ottomans of all periods. The same tradition emphasizing personalities in historical scholarship seems to have been continued in republican Turkey, judging from the biographical notes on various officials appended to the general histories of İ. H. Uzunçarşılı and İ. H. Danişmend.[13]

All these works, and other biographical collections on poets, learned men, prominent men of different regions, provide material of considerable wealth for prosopographic research. It is probably because most of this material is concerned with members of the learned profession that modern Ottoman specialists working on group biographies have largely concentrated on the *ulemā*. For the other groups in the Ottoman establishment the most detailed source is the *Sicill-i Osmāni*, which presents some problems. Although this work aims to be comprehensive it leaves out a large number of prominent Ottomans, especially of the earlier periods. Again, mostly for the earlier periods, the biographical notes for each entry are usually no more than a few lines; the scanty information provided is also often wrong in one way or another. In view of the defective character of *Sicill-i Osmāni*, for a sound and valid study it should be used only after it has been corrected and supplemented by information gleaned from other sources, such as chronicles and, wherever possible, archival documents.

Let us review further the general inadequacy of Ottoman sources for prosopographic research. Persons to be included in the *Sicill-i Osmāni*, or in any other biographical dictionary for that matter, are obviously the most successful men in a society; studies based on such sources can therefore deal only with the highest levels of that society. The common justification for the study of elites, of course, is that it is the ruling groups which play the dominant and most important role in the development of societies; it can therefore be argued that the proper study of a political order is its elite. But the fact that only the leading men are included in biographical compilations very often means that even the elite itself cannot be properly studied.

As an illustration of this point assume that most Ottomans to be elevated to the post of *beylerbeyi* (governor-general) had been trained in the palace school (*enderūn*). This would indicate the importance of a palace training for advancements in the ranks of the *seyfiye* (military-administrative) career, that it is a necessary condition of such advancement. But when we consider the sufficient conditions, we cannot evaluate the contribution of a palace education to advancement unless we know the proportion of the *enderūn* graduates who reach the position of *beylerbeyi* to their fellow students who remained at lower ranks. Furthermore even if we are able to determine other common characteristics of the *enderūn* graduates who become *beylerbeyi*s we would still need to know whether other palace-trained officers shared these characteristics. Let us further assume that most palace-trained *beylerbeyi*s also happened to be relatives or clients of highly placed Ottomans.

Since it is possible that other such well-connected *enderūn* graduates failed to reach the rank of *beylerbeyi*, we still would not be able to say whether connection with high Ottomans, in addition to a palace education, is a sufficient condition of advancement to the highest military-administrative posts. In short, to be able to analyze the achievements of top-ranking officials we also need to know about others who started life in similar circumstances but who failed to achieve the same success.

All this may be said to be self-evident. It is an age-old problem that one has to define failure in order to be able to define success or, to put it in even more general terms, to comprehend opposites in terms of each other. In literature the problem is resolved by the author, as Laertes is created, for example, as a foil to Hamlet. In historical research, too, the problem has significant implications. The success of the Ottoman emirate in creating an empire is better appreciated only after a consideration of other emirates of fourteenth-century Anatolia that did not achieve a similar development. But most sources of historical research, chronicles as well as biographical compilations, deal with successful persons or societies, neglecting the failures. Thus, the importance of archival documents is enhanced because they allow the researcher at least a degree of familiarity with groups below the highest ranks.

Biographical dictionaries in general and the *Sicill-i Osmāni* in particular are inadequate for yet another reason: there is next to no information on the early stages of the development of an individual in these sources. The data given is limited to his later career; it is almost impossible to determine how exactly he was educated or trained, what steps he took, what progress he made, or even what age he was when he held a particular position.

Furthermore, we cannot talk of a tradition of writing auto-biographies or memoirs in the Ottoman cultural world. Among the rare exceptions can be mentioned the verse autobiography of Varvar Ali Paşa, a seventeenth-century vezir which, although short (177 couplets), nevertheless supplies information not to be found in other sources.[15] The famous *Travels* of Evliya Çelebi, too, can be considered memoirs as well as travel notes: the author gives extensive information on his own life as well as on prominent Ottomans of the mid-seventeenth century.[16] Evliya Çelebi's biography is important for my purposes because he is a middle-level Ottoman, an example of the "relative failures" among Ottoman officials. For the same reason Katib Çelebi's autobiographical notes are interesting: they illuminate the development not only of a major scholar, but also of a middle-level bureaucrat, though admittedly not a very typical one.[17] Such autobiographical notes, however, remain as exceptions in the general dearth of materials on early lives of prominent Ottomans.

Further Definition of the Topic

Because of the inadequacy of general sources for a group-biographical study, and specifically to be able to penetrate below the upper strata of Ottoman society, I concentrated my research on archival sources. Among the documents I was able to discover were four *beylerbeyi* and *sancakbeyi* (district governor) appointment registers which, because they fell exactly within the time limit I had set and also because they provided data suitable for statistical analysis, led me to direct my study toward Ottoman provincial administrators.

These registers and the way I exploited them are described in detail in appendix 2; nevertheless I would like to point out their basic features at the outset as the data they provide form the backbone of this study. The last two of the four appointment registers are from the same period; they supplement each other and should be considered together: we have, thus, material on three different periods. The first register covers the years 1568 to 1574 (975–982 A.H.) and the second 1578 to 1588 (986–996); the third and fourth, combined, extend from 1632 to 1641 (1041–1051). The registers are basically lists of the provinces and the districts of the empire with entries to show the appointments made to each province and district during the period covered by each register. In each entry in addition to the appointee's name and date of appointment there usually is information on the previous position he held and on the income allotted to him. The various posts an individual held can be traced through the register; we can thus determine the length of his tenure at each post, any time he spent out of office in between appointments, the geographical extent of his appointments within the empire, and the position he held at the time he was elevated to the rank of *sancakbeyi* or *beylerbeyi*. Since the registers cover the periods just before and after 1600, we are able to trace any changes in provincial administration careers right through this crucial period of overall transformation.

My original hope was to be able to integrate the data provided in the provincial appointment registers with information gleaned from chronicles and the *Sicill-i Osmāni*. This hope was dashed, however, for several reasons. For one thing, persons who did not rise above the rank of *sancakbeyi* or even of *beylerbeyi* were usually not sufficiently important to be included in the *Sicill-i Osmāni*, and they were rarely mentioned in the chronicles. When they were, more likely than not they were referred to as "Mehmed Bey" or "Ahmed Bey"; one is left completely in the dark as to which of the dozens of Mehmed or Ahmed Beys serving as governors at any given time was meant. Thus, even the meager information that one might extract from the chronicles is utterly useless as it cannot be related to specific persons noted in the archival registers. Furthermore, even when a particular Mehmed Bey (say "son of Ferhad Paşa") can be identified in both the appointment register and in the *Sicill-i Osmāni*, it is exceedingly rare that the information from various sources on the same person can be integrated in any meaningful way (see appendix 4, Career Samples).

In view of this situation, in this study I had to employ both major types of prosopographic approach: for some of the questions posed the answer is provided by the data extracted from the appointment registers and analyzed statistically; in the case of other questions, such as the economic position of the *ümerā* and changing patterns of recruitment into the palace, where there is no large body of standardized data on which to base the answers, I had to rely on the limited number of examples supplied by the chronicles and by archival documents other than the appointment registers, thus shifting from a statistical to an impressionistic explanation. I might add that there are still further questions that I did not even attempt to answer, however impressionistically: family life and cultural interests of the Ottoman man of the sword are just two examples of such questions that remain unanswered, at least for now.

Abbreviations

BA	Prime Minister's Archives, Istanbul
Cev. Dah.	Cevdet Catalogue, Internal Affairs
KK	Kamil Kepeci Catalogue
MAD	Maliyeden Müdevver Catalogue
TD	Tahrīr Registers
TSA	Topkapı Palace Archives
TSK	Topkapı Palace Library
Belgeler	*Belgeler, Türk Tarih Belgeleri Dergisi*
BSOAS	*Bulletin of the School of Oriental and African Studies*
EI (1)	*Encyclopedia of Islam*, 1st edition
EI (2)	*Encyclopedia of Islam*, 2d edition
İA	*İslam Ansiklopedisi*
İFM	*İktisat Fakültesi Mecmuası*
IJMES	*International Journal of Middle East Studies*
JAOS	*Journal of the American Oriental Society*
JESHO	*Journal of the Economic and Social History of the Orient*
TAD	*Tarih Araştırmaları Dergisi*
TD	*Tarih Dergisi*

Note on Transcription and Pronunciation

For the transcription of Ottoman terms and texts I have used modern Turkish spelling while trying to preserve the flavor of the original. Important texts are given in plates for the specialist. The pronunciation of the following Turkish letters may be unfamiliar to the English-speaking reader:

c	j, as in *j*am
ç	ch, as in *ch*ip
ğ	lengthens preceding vowel
ı	as the o in kingd*o*m, or the e in heav*e*n
j	zh, as in vi*s*ion
ö	like the German ö or oe
ş	sh, as in *sh*ip
ü	like the German ü or ue

The Sultan's Servants

CHAPTER 1

The Emergence
of the Ottoman State

THE OTTOMAN STATE emerged at the close of the thirteenth century on the Selçuklu-Byzantine frontier in northwest Anatolia at a point where the plateau descends to the coastal plains surrounding the Marmara Sea. It was only one of a number of frontier states, all with similar ethnic and social admixtures and similar rudimentary political structures, that came into being at about the same time around the rim of the Anatolian plateau along the Black Sea, the Aegean, and the Mediterranean.[1]

Turbulent social and political conditions on either side of the Selçuklu-Byzantine frontier in the second half of the thirteenth century facilitated the emergence of these autonomous mini-states. In the middle of the century the establishment of the Ilhāni state, the middle eastern branch of Jenghiz Khan's Mongol world empire with its center in northwestern Iran, had reduced the previously flourishing Anatolian Selçuklus of Konya to the status of a vassal, with little central authority. Furthermore, the Mongol onslaught had been preceded and accompanied by the movement of Turks, both sedentary and tribesmen (*türkmen*), into various parts of the middle east, especially into Anatolia. The Selçuklu administration, following age-old practice, encouraged these newcomers to settle in the frontier regions where they would least disrupt the society and economy of the interior and where their warlike quality, directed against the Byzantines, would be most effective. Toward the end of the century, while the Selçuklu administration was becoming more and more an Ilhāni satellite, the frontier regions grew more populous and less answerable to a central authority.

On the Byzantine side of the frontier, too, resistance to the growing pressure of Selçuklu frontiersmen was lacking. The restoration of Byzantine rule to Constantinople after the expulsion of the remnants of the Crusaders (1261) resulted in a greater degree of Byzantine involvement in Balkan affairs while western Anatolia, so vital during the Nicean period, declined in relative importance. Stability of the Byzantine-Selçuklu frontier had been carefully cultivated by both states earlier. But now, with Konya reduced and Constantinople preoccupied, leaders of Selçuklu frontiersmen seized the opportunity to establish themselves as independent rulers while respecting the distant suzerainty of the Ilhani overlords.

At first such mini-states (*beylik*) emerged on territories gained from Byzantine control, but others followed in the hinterland as the last vestiges of a central Selçuklu state disappeared. By the early fourteenth century all of Anatolia, including the central plateau, was divided among more than a dozen *beylik*s. Similar in social makeup and institutions, these *beylik*s were differentiated by the names of the persons or families who founded them, some of whom had been officials of the Selçuklu or the Ilhāni states and some leaders of tribal groups or of bands of frontiersmen.

Osman Bey, the eponymous leader of a relatively small group of frontiersmen around 1300, may have been the descendant of a family of tribal leaders. The fact that his community was called "Osmanlı," the followers of Osman, indicates that he established a new group, a new "tribe," so to speak, out of a mixture of *türkmen* tribesmen, peasants, and townsfolk, both Byzantines and Turks, when he set out to stake his own autonomous rule at the northwestern corner of the Anatolian plateau.[2] Under his leadership the band of Osman flourished by continuous raids into Byzantine territory to the west and north. The year Osman Bey died, probably 1324, also marked the capture of Bursa, the first sizable town to come under Osmanlı rule.

For the next thirty-five years Osman's son, Orhan Bey, ruled over an ever-expanding state and a society increasingly differentiated, heterogeneous, and sophisticated. Behind the frontiersmen pushing farther into Byzantine lands, Bursa flourished as an interregional trade and manufacturing center; schools and colleges (*medrese*) were established; more of the population, now that the plains had become Osmanlı territory, was engaged in agriculture. In addition to individuals and bands pouring in from the Anatolian interior to take part in frontier raids, learned men, bureaucrats and preachers, and other townsfolk, merchants and artisans, also came to become Osmanlıs.

To the west of Ottoman lands, extending to the Dardanelles, was another Turkish *beylik*, the Karesi. Taking advantage of a struggle among Karesi princes for the seat of *bey*—throne would be too grand a term—Orhan Bey extended his influence and gradually his rule over his neighbors. Around the middle of the century, all Karesi people, princes, officials, and commoners, had been assimilated into the "nation of Osman." The way was then open for the next step, across the Dardanelles and onto the European continent.

Once Orhan Bey came to control the passage to the Balkans, the influx of people, frontier fighters as well as sedentary folk, joining the Osmanlı enterprise grew even larger. As Osmanlı rule was extended in Thrace and the Ottoman *beys* increased their power, wealth, and prestige, other Turkish lands in Anatolia were also absorbed, mostly through peaceful means. Ottomans bought some lands from neighboring Turkish princes, and received territory as wedding gifts when marital ties were formed with other ruling houses. Through most of the fourteenth century the Ottomans used little force in extending their rule in Anatolia, but in the last decade of the century the fourth *bey*, Yıldırım (the Thunderbolt) Bayezid, conducted a policy of forceful unification of Anatolia under his rule. By 1400, Ottoman domains extended from Serbia in the west and the Danube in the north in the Balkans to include western and northern Anatolia. The Osmanlı enterprise had grown in the course of a century from a band of frontiersmen into a state of considerable size and power.

Early Development of Ottoman Administration

With the growth of the state in size and maturity, political, administrative, and social institutions were introduced, modeled for the most part on those of the Selçuklu state.[3] The basic military character of the state, in the initial frontiersmen's enterprise as well as in the extensive territorial state, predominated as in other middle eastern states in the post-Mongol period. At first almost all male Osmanlıs joined the frontier raids and attacks; Osman's band was a veritable miniature citizen's army. As Osman's followers moved out of the frontier zone and began to control a larger territory, there was a growing number of peasants and townsmen not involved in the fighting. Thus there came about a differentiation between the fighters, the military men, called *askeri*, and the *reāyā*, the subjects. Some of the fighters went with the frontier as it moved north and west, and then across the Dardanelles into Thrace. Such men who were constantly on the borders, the frontiersmen, were called *akıncı*, the raiders; they lived on the fruits of their raids into infidel territory and perhaps also (definitely later on) on tax revenues of the frontier zones allotted to them. Some others of the military men remained in the Ottoman hinterland; they joined the bey's campaigns whenever they were summoned, but the rest of the time they remained dispersed throughout the countryside, charged with maintaining order in towns and villages where they resided. In return for such services, the bey allowed them to collect for themselves tax revenues of their localities. Thus emerged the classical system of provincial administration, the cornerstone of Ottoman government until 1600, with its military, administrative, and financial aspects.

The position of the Ottoman bey, too, changed in the course of the fourteenth century. Osman Bey had been a first among equals, the leader of a modest band of frontiersmen. His residence in the small town of Söğüt could not have been too opulent and was probably not much bigger than other households. Like others in his band, his wealth consisted of a herd of sheep and a few slaves.[4] By the end of the century his great-grandson, Bayezid I, was styled not *bey* but sultan, a much more exalted title, symbolizing his passage from mere leader to firm ruler. Bayezid had palaces in Bursa and in Edirne. The central institutions of the state, a chancery and a financial bureaucracy, had developed as extensions of his household, in addition to his household troops, the central army of his state. The Ottoman sultan was as much a military commander in 1400 (indeed remained so for centuries) as Osman Bey had been when he led his band of frontiersmen.

From the earliest days there had been need for learned men (ulema in the plural) not only to teach in the new Ottoman colleges (*medrese*) but also to serve as judges (*kadı*), applying the precepts of Islamic law (*şeriat*) and features of local custom and usages, and as supervisors of town markets. The highest judge, the *kadıasker*, remained near the sultan and was sometimes elevated to the rank of *vezir*, a counselor to the sultan. In its early development the Ottoman state thus conformed more closely to the earlier Islamic models where the vezir was a chief bureaucrat and political advisor: a man of learning best exemplified by Nizām ül-Mülk, the famous eleventh-century vezir of the Great Selçuklus, guiding the sultan who was essentially the commander-in-chief of the armies, the supreme military commander.

Balancing the *kadıasker*, there also emerged the office of *beylerbeyi*, supreme commander of provincial forces. This office became essential, as the Ottoman state was increasingly engaged on two fronts, the Balkans and Anatolia: while the sultan as commander-in-chief was leading Ottoman armies to battle on one front the *beylerbeyi* guarded the other. More often, however, the *beylerbeyi* was the active commander, especially in the Balkans (*Rumeli*, in Ottoman parlance), while the sultan resided in Bursa. Towards the end of the fourteenth century, as a result of the sudden enlargement of Ottoman territories in Anatolia, a second *beylerbeyi* was created. The office, which had been a general one, for the whole state, became territorialized: there was now one *beylerbeyi* for Rumeli and another for Anatolia, and they in time became governors general for their regions. Soon followed a third *beylerbeyi*, this time for the north-central Anatolia region conquered at the very end of the century, called the province (*vilāyet*) of Rum, centered at Sivas. The other two *beylerbeyi* resided at Sofia in Rumeli and at

Ankara, and later more often at Kütahya, in western Anatolia.[5]

Increasingly in the course of the fifteenth century and especially during the reign of Mehmed II (r. 1451–81), the military governors general were promoted to the office of vezir almost exclusively, though a rare learned bureaucrat vezir is still occasionally encountered as late as the early sixteenth century. The political-legal vezir of 1400 had become a political-military official, the sultan's absolute deputy as commander and chief administrator, by 1500.[6] Indeed, in addition to the grand vezir, there were other vezirs at the capital, all from the military-administrative career. The vezirs were members of the sultan's council (*divān-ı humāyūn*) which also included the two *kadıasker*s, the head of the financial bureau (*defterdar*) and the head of the chancery (*nişancı*). The council, under the direction of the sultan or, in his absence, of the grand vezir, deliberated on all matters of state, political and administrative, as well as serving as the high court of appeals, to which all subjects had access in principle.

The Sultan's Household

The elevation of the role of the bey/sultan in Ottoman polity had as its main component the creation of an extensive household. Osman Bey's modest establishment of a herd of sheep and a handful of slaves and servants had given way, by 1400, to palaces in Edirne and Bursa where hundreds of slaves attended to the sultan's needs. The royal household had an inner section (*enderūn*) where palace pages served the sultan's person while being in training for positions in the outer section (*bīrūn*).[7] In the *bīrūn* organization the pages became, to give a few illustrations, palace gatekeepers (*kapıcı*), pursuivants (*çavuş*), officers of the stables (*emīrahur*) and the royal band of musicians and of the tentsetters (*emīralem*). Such *bīrūn* officials, as well as performing the duties indicated by their titles, also served as the sultan's messengers and envoys to the provinces or even abroad. The most important officers of outer palace organization were the commanders of the various corps of the standing army, collectively called the *kapıkulu*, household troops. The *kapıkulu* consisted originally of the infantry, *yeniçeri* (janissary), and regiments of the household cavalry, to which were added, in the course of the fifteenth century, armourers (*cebeci*), cannoneers (*topçu*) and cannon-carriagemen (*top arabacıları*). Around 1450 the sultan's household troops numbered several thousand and the musket-bearing *yeniçeri* had already gained fame as a formidable force both in the Balkans and in eastern Anatolia.

The household troops, indeed almost the whole of the sultan's household, was made up of slaves. In this, as in most other institutions, the Ottomans followed Islamic near-eastern states: from the eighth century on specially trained slaves from beyond the domains of Islam had formed the backbone of central armies from Bagdad to Andalusia, from Cairo to Delhi. Even in the earliest days of Osman's enterprise the bey's household included some slaves who served as military aids. In the second half of the fourteenth century, as the Ottoman bey tried to elevate his position in society vis-à-vis other leaders, especially those directing the raids of the *akıncı* in the Balkans, he undertook to enlarge his household. He claimed for himself one-fifth of the booty of his troops as bey's right, to be paid either as one-fifth of the value, or, in the case of prisoners of war and other captives, by surrendering one out of five to the bey. These slaves were formed into the "new troops," *yeniçeri* in Turkish and rendered janissary by Europeans, the sultan's household troops and the first standing army of the state.

For reasons still not clear but possibly having to do with the syncretic mood of a frontier zone, by the end of the century the Ottoman sultan started the practice, called *devşirme*, literally "gathering," of recruiting the sturdy sons of his own non-Muslim subjects to serve in his household. These boys became Muslims, learned Turkish, and were trained to become soldiers; those who were good-looking and seemed capable were admitted to the palace inner service (*enderūn*), given a well-rounded education and training, and, after a number of years, were sent forth from the palace to join the household cavalry regiments or other outer palace (*bīrūn*) corps, and sometimes directly to take up positions in provincial administration. The longer a page served in the *enderūn*, the higher the position he achieved in the *bīrūn* or in the provinces.

The sultan's slaves sent out to serve in provincial administration joined there men who held positions because their fathers were Ottoman officials, or who had served in other households, or even those who had risen from *reāyā*, subject status, by volunteering to serve in the sultan's campaigns.

CHAPTER 2

Provincial Administration

THE OTTOMAN TERM for provincial administration, *dirlik*, is a very telling one. *Dirlik* literally means livelihood, illustrating the essential point of the system, that is, that it provided income for officers, who performed duties for the state. *Dirlik* denotes the state revenues in a particular locality allocated to an official; in the process of collecting those revenues from the sultan's subjects the official supervised cultivation and other economic activities and also maintained public order in his particular locality. Part of his revenues consisted of fines collected for various crimes and transgressions. Most *dirlik* holders were military men; their primary obligation to the state was to take part in the sultan's campaigns, paying for their expenses from the proceeds of their *dirlik*. The *dirlik* system, then, was a system of tax collection, provided peace and security in the provinces, and supported the main body of the Ottoman army.

Inasmuch as the officers of the *dirlik* system, from the lowest-grade *timar* holder to the *beylerbeyi*, the provincial governor, were military men, there also existed what may be called a parallel and separate system of provincial administration. This second system was a legal-administrative one, manned by graduates of the *medreses*, colleges of religion and religious law. Various grades of these magistrates (*kadı*) were assigned to different size communities, but not in a hierarchical arrangement. Thus there were *kadı*s in cities which were seats of provinces and districts, in towns

Warsaw•

Poland •Lublin

Kiev

•Cracow

Danube R.   Vienna

•Paris

France   Hapsburg
          Empire

Drava R.

Venice•   KANISZA

EGER
BUDIN
•Budin   TIMIŞVAR

Dniester

MOLDAVIA

TRANSYL-
VANIA

Sava R.   •Belgrade   WALLACHIA

BOSNIA   ÖZI

•Madrid

Spain   •Rome   RUMELI   •Sofia   Edirne
                                      Istanbul

•Cordoba   Salonica•

Granada•   AEGEAN
            ISLANDS   Iz

Algiers•   Tunis•
ALGIERS   TUNIS

MEDITERRANEAN

Tripoli•
TRIPOLI   Al

OTTOMAN PROVINCES
c. 1650

Mi. 0   200   400   600   800

Km. 0   200   400   600   800

where a *zaīm* or *subaşı* commanded, and in larger villages, all appointed by the *kadıaskers* at the center and all directly responsible to Istanbul. In addition to applying the *şeriat*, Muslim law, in civil and commercial cases, the *kadıs* administered criminal law as it emanated from the sultan. The *kadıs* also received and entered in their local court registers all imperial fermans and administrative rules and regulations. The execution of at least a portion of such orders was left in their hands. They were also charged with ensuring that correct procedures were followed by other officers. The *kadıs*, as well as the *dirlik* officers, were notified of the arrival in their locality of officials from Istanbul and were asked to facilitate the performance of their various tasks, from tax collection to special investigations. In many cases, especially in the application of criminal law, the magistrates and the *dirlik* officers cooperated, even collaborated. Basically, however, they represented two different traditions, the military and the legal, and operated in different spheres.

*Dirlik*s came in different sizes, according to the rank and position of the officers receiving them. It is customary to classify *dirlik*s according to their yield: a *timar* produced revenues up to 20,000 *akçe*s; a *zeāmet* from 20,000 to 100,000 *akçe*s; a *dirlik* with revenues above 100,000 *akçe*s was called a *hās*. While this classification is used in all standard works on Ottoman history, it is unsatisfactory. For one thing, the limits of yield for each type of *dirlik* seem to have crystallized only in the sixteenth century; for earlier periods the registers report *zeāmet*s yielding less than, or *timar*s with revenues greater than, 20,000 *akçe*s.[1] Indeed, in addition to meaning the smallest *dirlik* grant, the term *timar* was also used in a general sense, as a synonym for *dirlik*.[2]

Consideration of the original meanings of the terms used for different levels of *dirlik*s and establishing their functional differentiation will present a clearer picture. *Timar* means horse-grooming; by extension it came to denote revenues sufficient for any cavalryman but especially one who was otherwise untitled and without rank.[3] As it was given to the lowest grade of provincial cavalrymen, a *timar* was the smallest in yield and consisted of village-level revenues.[4] *Zeāmet*, on the other hand, was granted to a *zaīm*, a commander; it was a *dirlik* that supported a middle-level officer who deserved a larger grant, made up of town-level revenues, but also including rural revenues from areas around the towns. The *zeāmet* holder, it follows, was a town commander, *subaşı* in Turkish.[5] Finally, *hās* means 'set aside for,' 'reserved for.' These were the largest groupings of revenues granted to the highest ranking officials, not only the *beylerbeyi* (province governor) and *sancakbeyi* (district governor) in provincial administration, but also to vezirs at the capital. Provincial revenues reserved for the sultan himself were termed *havāss-ı humāyūn*, imperial reserves. Sources of highly concentrated tax revenues were included in the *hās*, specifically all urban revenues not devoted to *vakıf*s. Customs receipts of the most important ports and yields of all mining operations were reserved for the sultan's *hās*.

Functionally, aside from the type of revenue source in terms of settlement size, there was an even more basic distinction between *timar* and *zeāmet* on one hand and the *hās* on the other. *Timar*s and *zeāmet*s were self-contained units in an administrative sense; the authority of the *timar* or *zeāmet* holder was coextensive with the limits of his *dirlik*. There was no hierarchical relationship between the two; that is, the *zeāmet* was essentially a larger *timar* and the *zaīm* had no authority over holders of lesser *dirlik*s. For a *zaīm* or a *timar* holder his *dirlik* and his office were the same.

A *hās*, however, was not an office, but merely the revenues allocated for a particular office, the authority of which went beyond the limits of the *dirlik* and included in its purview lesser offices and *dirlik*s. At the top the sultan, for example, had his own imperial *hās*, but he was obviously the ruler of the whole empire. The *beylerbeyi* had his *hās* concentrated mostly in one district (*sancak*) of his province, the governor's seat, but his authority extended throughout the province. So also the *sancakbeyi*, the district governor, had only a portion of his district's revenues allocated to him as his *hās* but was the governor of the whole district. In terms of administration, the correspondance between *dirlik*, source of revenue, and office disappeared at the *sancak* level. On one hand a *sancak* (district) included lesser *dirlik*s within its boundaries; on the other hand larger administrative divisions, provinces, were made up of groups of *sancak*s; it is in this sense that the *sancak* was the basic unit of provincial administration.[6]

The *Sancak*

The original meaning of the term *sancak* is "banner" or "standard" and, by extension, "command." Even when the term came to be applied to a particular region, it was used in the sense of command of that distinct. The *sancakbeyi*, district governor, was primarily the commander of the provincial cavalry, the *dirlik* holders of his district. Indeed, especially in the earlier centuries, the same officer was sometimes mentioned specifically as "*atlu sancakbeyi*," cavalry commander.[7] As late as the fifteenth century when the primary connotation of *sancak* had become administrative district, we find the term used to refer to the provincial troops in various districts.[8]

As administrative districts, *sancak* boundaries reflected pre-Ottoman administrative divisions and geographical realities. The number of *sancak*s has remained remarkably stable through the centuries, even into republican times. The number of *vilāyet*s (provinces) in modern Turkey, especially in western and northern Anatolia, is practically the same as the number of *sancak*s in fifteenth-century Anatolia.

An Ottoman *sancak* was a district encompassing, at a rough estimate, an area of several thousand square miles and a population of perhaps a hundred thousand on the average. Although the figures varied considerably from one *sancak* to another, a district included about a dozen *zeāmet*s and perhaps a hundred *timar*s.

The significance of the *sancak* as an administrative unit is best illustrated by the fact that provincial regulations (*kānūnnāme*s) were prepared separately for each *sancak*, and each *sancak* was the subject of provincial cadastral surveys.[9] When a new *sancak* was established, a list of regulations, mainly dealing with tax rates, market dues, and other fees, was drawn up. Often the regulations took into account conditions and practices existing in that region before Ottoman conquest. In other cases standard Ottoman practice was introduced to the newly established *sancak*. Increasingly in the sixteenth century, when a typically Ottoman set of regulations came to be recognized, there was a sustained effort to discourage varying local customs in order to achieve a greater degree of consistency from one region to the next. In some cases the *kānūnnāme* stated that the new subjects specifically asked that Ottoman rules and regulations by applied to them rather than maintain earlier usages.[10] Also in the sixteenth century, when fairly extensive territories were conquered all at once, and possibly also with a view to eliminating local variations, a single *kānūnnāme* was issued for a group of *sancak*s. Thus, for example, there was one *kānūnnāme* for all the *sancak*s of the province of Erzurum, and at the other extreme of the empire one for four *sancak*s of Hungary.[11]

An economic survey (*tahrīr*) of the district was next drawn up, listing all the human and economic resources, town by town, village by village. On the basis of the rates indicated in the *kānūnnāme* and the population and production figures obtained in the economic survey, the tax liability of persons and communities were estimated and entered in the *tahrīr* registers. These detailed (*mufassal*) registers, which specified what the state could expect to receive from her subjects, then formed the basis for another type of register, the summary (*icmāl*, or sometimes *mücmel*) register, showing how the state revenues were to be apportioned. The *icmal* registers, in other words, listed all the *dirlik*s of the *sancak*, from the *hās* allocated to the *sancakbeyi*, to the *zeāmet*s and *timar*s. If the *sancak* was a productive one, it could include imperial *dirlik*s (*havāss-ı humāyūn*) and revenues forming part of the governor general's (*beylerbeyi*) *hās*, in addition to what he received in his own *sancak*, the seat of the province.

It was noted above that while in the case of *timar*s and *zeāmet*s the *dirlik* and the office were coextensive, in the case of *hās* the authority of the office went beyond the boundaries of the areas allotted to the *dirlik* of the high-level officer. In the *hās* of the *sancakbeyi*, however, were included the revenues not only of specific cities, towns, and rural areas, but also some revenues which originated in all parts of his district. Thus the correlation between *dirlik* and office was preserved, although to a lesser extent than in the case of smaller *dirlik*s. A consideration of the constituent parts of a *sancakbeyi*'s *hās*, therefore, might shed some light on the nature of the authority of district governors.

The *Sancakbeyi* and His *Hās*

At the outset we have to clear a problem concerning official revenues allotted to *sancakbeyi*s. Obviously, different *sancakbeyi*s deserved and were given different levels of revenue. An officer just promoted to *sancakbeyi* rank usually received 150,000 *akçe*s in annual revenue; around the middle of the sixteenth century this minimum seems to have been raised to 200,000 *akçe*s. Through the years the *sancakbeyi* received raises as he was moved to different *sancak*s. He also received merit raises, usually on the occasion of extraordinary effectiveness in campaigns, while he was at the same post. Both seniority and merit raises came to roughly 10 percent of the officer's revenues. A senior *sancakbeyi*, after a fairly long career at that rank, received 500,000 or 600,000 *akçe*s per year.

*Sancak*s, too, varied in prosperity, productivity, and strategic importance. Certain *sancak*s, such as Kırkkilise in Thrace and Kocaeli in northwestern Anatolia, were usually granted with low-level *hās* yields, about 200,000 *akçe*s, while Bosna and Silistre, for example, both in the Balkans, were granted with *hās* revenues of more than 500,000 *akçe*s. Obviously junior *sancakbeyi*s were appointed to *sancak*s on the order of Kırkkilise and Kocaeli, while the most experienced and highly regarded officers were rewarded with appointments to the like of Bosna and Silistre. Between these two extremes, however, were most *sancak*s which differed little from one another. One *sancakbeyi* might hold the *sancak* of Vidin, for example, at 300,000 *akçe*s and he might be shifted to Kayseri at 320,000 *akçe*s. The previous governor of Kayseri might have been receiving only 250,000 *akçe*s, and, if it happened that he was then appointed to Vidin, he might still receive the same amount. To continue with our illustration, the new appointee to Vidin might receive a merit raise a year later and then hold the same *sancak* at an increased revenue, say 270,000 *akçe*s. In most cases, in other words, the *hās* of the *sancakbeyi* depended on what the person deserved and less on the *sancak*, with the obvious exceptions of the least and the most important *sancak*s.

The problem should by now be evident. Inasmuch as the same *sancak* was granted to different *bey*s with varying *hās* revenues, since the amount of the *hās* was determined according to the appointee and not according to the post, how can we treat *sancakbeyi* revenues at particular posts in any systematic manner?[12] How can we hope to establish the component parts of a *sancakbeyi hās* if the figure is capable of changing from one appointee to another, indeed even for the same person from one year to the next?

In theory the problem can be resolved once we ascertain that indeed in each *sancak* there were revenues set aside for the governor, whoever he might be. If he deserved more than this standard amount, such specific revenues might be augmented. It might even be that most appointees to a district received more than was reserved in that *sancak* for the governor. Still, there was a core portion in each *sancak* specific to the governors appointed there. This core portion was usually called *sancak hāsılı*, literally the yield of the *sancak*, obviously not meaning all revenues generated in that district but those revenues reserved for the district governor, even though his total *hās* might be larger.

That there existed a "yield of the district" reserved for appointees to a particular post needs to be documented. Mention must be made, because it has been published and is quoted widely, of Ayni Ali's report on Ottoman provincial administration where the *hās* in each *sancak* is listed (see appendix 1). This work, however, dates from the early seventeenth century when the system of provincial administration was in flux; furthermore, the author consulted registers much earlier than his time to prepare his report. Evidence should be drawn fresh, from earlier sources.

The expression used in the earliest surviving provincial register, dating from 1431, implies that there was a *hās* reserved for the governor, but it may not be deemed conclusive.[13] For more specific references let us consider several consecutive appointments to Kayseri *sancak*, entered in the late-fifteenth-century *dirlik* grant register, MAD 17893. The first appointee (p. 26) was a Kasım Bey, son of Hızır Paşa, whose total *hās* was increased to 405,881 *akçe*s with additions to the standard yield (the expression used here is *hāshā-ı livā*) of 250,575 *akçe*s. Shortly thereafter a Mehmed Bey was appointed to Kayseri (p. 26) but the *hās* figure was not entered. Again a short time later Mehmed Bey was dismissed because he was infirm (*malūl*) and the *sancak* was granted to Sinan Bey, tutor (*lala*) of prince Sultan Ahmed (p. 46). The district's yield (here *hāsıl-ı livā*) of 250,575 was augmented to 372,335 *akçe*s for Sinan Bey. For the next two appointments (pp. 176 and 248) only the names of the appointees and the total *hās* of 400,000 *akçe*s are entered; the standard yield is not specified.

A further example is drawn from a governor's appointment register, KK 262, dating from the 1580s.[14] The *sancak* of Prizrin was granted to Hızır Bey, who had previously held Vılçitrin district with revenues of 340,620 *akçe*s; he took out an imperial diploma of office (*berāt*) at his new post, which specified that the standard *hās* of Prizrin amounting to 281,642 *akçe*s had been augmented to 348,610 *akçe*s in his case (*livā-ı mezbūrun [Prizrin] 281,642 akçelik hāslarɪ[n] ber vech-i tekmil 348,610 akçe ile berāt eyledi*). These examples establish that the standard yield of Kayseri around 1485 was 250,575 *akçe*s and that of Prizrin around 1580 was 281,642 *akçe*s, although the *hās* granted a specific *sancakbeyi* might be much higher, about 25 percent in the Prizrin example and as much as 60 percent in Kayseri, to bring the standard yield to a level commensurate with what each appointee personally deserved.

It is the standard yield of a *sancak*, not the *hās* granted a particular holder of that post, that should ideally form the basis for a consideration of district governors' revenues as an indication of their authority. Having said this, I have to admit it cannot be done, for it is practically impossible to determine the component parts of the standard yield in a sufficient number of cases to allow a meaningful statistical analysis. We can tell, from the examples cited above, that the *sancak hāsıl*, the core portion of the revenues granted to all incumbents at a certain *sancak*, did exist, but its composition is not given. Even in *icmāl defter*s, the summary district registers that enumerate all the *dirlik* grants in a *sancak*, the *hās* entered for the *sancakbeyi* is not the standard yield but all revenues allocated to the particular governor in office at the time the register was drawn up.

It is true that in some *icmāl* registers the *hās* is recorded in two sections, the first labeled *hāshā-ı kadīm* (old *hās*) and the second *hāshā-ı cedīd* (new *hās*) or simply "additions" (*ilhāk*). A study of how a *hās* changes, however, shows that *hāshā-ı kadīm* is not the same as the standard yield (*sancak hāsılı*) but only the *hās* held by the previous appointee, the existing *hās*, which may be changed according to the figure the new appointee is to be allotted. The *hās* given in appendix 3 may serve as an example in this context.

There we note that when Murad Bey was appointed *sancakbeyi* of Alacahisar (Kruşevaç in Macedonia), he was given a raise of 30,000 *akçe*s over the existing *hās*, labeled *hāshā-ı kadīm*, of 218,980 *akçe*s bringing the total to 252,180. About a year later Murad Bey deserved a merit raise of another 30,000 *akçe*s, thus his income went up to 280,000 *akçe*s. However, in the process Murad Bey also requested and was granted some changes in the original portion of his *hās*, the *hāshā-ı kadīm*. Two villages included in the *hāshā-ı kadīm*, complained Murad Bey, were too far from the other areas he held as parts of his *hās*, making tithing difficult. These two villages were taken out of the original portion of 218,980, bringing it down to 205,335 *akçe*s. The figure he held before the second raise, too, went down by the same amount; he held only 238, 835 from the *hāshā-ı kadīm*. In other words, both the original portion of 218,980 *akçe*s and the *hās*, before the second raise, of 252,180, were later referred as *hāshā-ı kadīm*. The conclusion is that *hāshā-ı kadīm* did not refer to any unchanging specific figure and therefore cannot be taken as a substitute for the standard yield of the district.

As the standard yield of Ottoman *sancak*s cannot be determined, we have to base our observations on the nature of the *sancakbeyi*'s *hās* on evidence more readily available, that is, on the *hās* entries in summary registers (*icmāl defter*s). As mentioned, such entries record actual grants to specific governors, including any raises they may have been given. Inasmuch as raises or other additions were usually made up of the revenues of villages in various parts of the *sancak*, the *hās* entries in district registers show a higher proportion of rural revenues than would the standard yields of districts, had we been able to ascertain them. Nevertheless, even this material shows conclusively that in an overwhelming majority of *sancak*s a very high percentage of the governor's *hās* consisted of urban revenues and certain revenues the governor collected throughout his *sancak*.[15] There were two types of exception. In some districts, mostly in Albania and in central Greece, where there simply were not many cities or towns, the percentage of rural revenues was obviously higher. Even in such districts, however, an effort was made to include the revenues of bigger villages in the *hās*. At the other extreme were highly urbanized *sancak*s like Halep (Aleppo), Alaiye, and Teke with important international commercial centers. In such areas the considerable customs levies and other urban revenues were included in the imperial reserves (*havāss-ı humāyūn*) or in the governor general's *hās* or both. In such cases, too, to supplement the urban revenues at the *sancakbeyi*'s disposal, revenues of relatively larger villages were allocated to him.

Convenience partially accounts for the fact that relatively bigger sources of revenue were set aside for holders of important offices. Obviously it would have been cumbersome for the sultan to have to receive his income from many towns and villages scattered throughout the empire; similarly the *sancakbeyi* and his men would have to spend too much time and effort to collect revenues, in small sums, from many different and far-flung villages.[16] But this would be a partial explanation only. Perhaps a more important consideration was that larger sources of revenue should remain undivided and in the control of a high-level official with sufficient authority to do this effectively. An urban source of revenue, the proceeds from various urban industries, for example, if divided into several *timar*s, would have no clear line of authority over it. But if that source of revenue were placed in the hands of the *sancakbeyi*, he could supervise the functioning of the economic activity that produced the tax revenue while collecting his revenue. Similarly, if the various revenues of an urban center were to be divided among several officials, the political authority in that town would be blurred.

Urban revenues were allocated to governors because, in addition to convenience in revenue collection, the highest official should control the biggest centers. The governor's authority in his district, then, was primarily exercised in relatively large centers, where he received revenues from the marketplace, port activities, bridge tolls, mills, and manufacturing establishments.[17] The head tax on non-Muslims (*cizye*), too, was sometimes left to the *sancakbeyi*.[18] Perhaps it is not surprising in a preindustrial society that taxes on agricultural produce in and near the city—on vineyards, orchards, vegetable patches, grain fields, and fisheries—constituted a significant portion of urban revenues. Another important category of income in urban centers consisted of various fines the governor collected in the process of keeping order and security in his district. Such revenues, called *niyābet*, comprised not only fines on crimes and transgressions (*cürm ve cināyet*), but also of incidental levies (*bād-ı havā*) such as fines for stray cattle and rewards for the apprehension of escaped slaves.

Niyābet revenues in amount were by no means the most substantial portion of the governor's income. It was rather the nature of *niyābet* revenues that made them important. The term *niyābet* literally means "deputyship," referring to the fact that the governors, indeed all officials of the *dirlik* system, were deputies of the sultan in the realm, representing his political authority in keeping internal security, especially through the apprehension and punishment of criminals. In one province of the empire, Karaman, originally one of the frontier *beyliks* of post-Selçuklu Anatolia and the last of such states to be incorporated into the Ottoman realm, having been finally conquered in the 1460s, with its relatively long independent existence as an area having regulations and official terminology somewhat different than those elsewhere in the lands then included in the empire, *niyābet* revenues were termed *ādet-i emīrāne*, governor's dues.[19] The term *emīrāne* is a much more direct reference to political authority than *niyābet*, and the identity of the real content of the two terms allows us to establish with certainty what exactly was meant by the "deputyship" expressed in *niyābet*.

The process of the collection of *niyābet* revenues or governor's dues is important in two other ways. The apprehension, prosecution, and punishment of criminals was a process in which the military-administrative authorities, officials of the *dirlik* system, were required to cooperate closely with the *kadıs*, the magistrates representing the sultan's legal authority. The military authorities brought suspects to court, the *kadıs* tried them in accordance with the sultan's law (*kānūn*), and punishment was administered by the *dirlik* officials. The two parallel systems thus complemented each other, as well as balancing each other's authority. Furthermore, the governor collected *niyābet* revenues not only in those areas, urban as well as rural, directly included in his *hās* but also elsewhere in his district, receiving half of the *niyābet* revenues collected in *timars* throughout his district. All *hās*, *zeāmets*, and certain bigger *timars*, those given to holders of specific military posts such as fortress commanders (*dizdār*) and troop leaders (*alaybeyi*), were termed "free" (*serbest*) in this respect: the holders collected and kept for themselves all *niyābet* dues in their *dirliks*. But the lesser *timar* holders, termed "non-free" (*gayr ez serbest*), shared equally their *niyābet* revenues with the district governor.[20] It should be pointed out that even in "free" *timars* the district governor retained the authority to investigate and punish in cases involving relatively serious crimes.[21] Such *niyābet* revenues the *sancakbeyi* received throughout the district, as opposed to those he collected within areas directly allocated to him, were termed *niyābet-i il*.

By inclusion of *niyābet-i il* within the governor's *hās*, an attempt was made to achieve some measure of correspondence between the office of governor and his *hās*, a correspondence which existed more fully for smaller *dirliks* and which is the underlying logic of the *dirlik* system. In other ways as well this correspondence was established for the *sancakbeyi*: at least in the fifteenth century the governor received a share of the basic tax on the landholding peasants, the yoke tax (*çift resmi*), again from non-free *timars*.[22] Finally, in areas where there were nomads in addition to the stable population, the various taxes and dues levied on the nomads accrued to the governor of the district rather than being apportioned among lesser *dirliks*. Because taxes on nomads had to be levied not on individuals but on groups, clans, or tribes, moving together, an official of high standing was needed to deal with them. And because the migration routes of nomadic groups took them through various parts of a district, even into several districts; this, too, brought them under the direct supervision of the district governor.

Through the revenues allocated to him, then, the governor came in direct contact with three groups of subjects: the urban and peasant population included in his *hās*; the *reāyā* of non-free *timars*, through sharing *niyābet* dues and the yoke tax; and the nomadic groups who lived within his district or who seasonally passed through it. The *reāyā* on lands included in other officials' *hās*, in *zeāmet*s, or in free *timar*s, on the other hand, were not subject to his authority, nor was the *reāyā* of freehold (*mülk*) or pious foundation (*vakf*) lands. It also happened sometimes that part of a governor's revenues accrued to him from holdings included in a different district; such holdings would be "free" vis-à-vis the governor of that district. Fairly rare until 1500, this situation became increasingly widespread in the course of the sixteenth century. We shall take up this development later; here it is sufficient to note that for a governor to have *hās* holdings in a different district goes directly against the logic of the *dirlik* system, which was to achieve as great a degree of correspondence as possible between a particular office and revenues allocated to the holder of that post.

Inasmuch as there was a body of *reāyā* not under the direct authority of a governor, the *dirlik* system cannot truly be considered provincial administration. The parallel system, through magistrates (*kadı*), was much more comprehensive in that it reached all the *reāyā* in more systematic fashion. In other words, while there may have been parts of a given district under the authority of a military official outside that district, in terms of the legal-administrative system the whole of the district was apportioned into subdivisions, called *kazā*, each under the purview of a particular *kadı*.[23]

Although a *sancakbeyi* may not have had direct dealings with all the subjects in his district, he had other administrative duties as part of his standing as governor of the whole district. He was obliged, for example, to assist government officials coming to his district from the center on special duty and to provide any facilities they might require.[24] The central government also asked governors, as representatives of the state, to undertake special investigations or to resolve various administrative, legal, or security problems.[25] It was the duty of governors of frontier districts to ensure that relations with neighboring states were conducted in accordance with existing agreements.[26] They could also carry out contacts with other states on their own initiative.[27]

As pointed out at the outset, the *dirlik* system was primarily a military organization, allowing for a provincial army of cavalry-men to be maintained efficiently on revenues, in cash and in kind, collected at the source. The position of the governors in Otto-man polity is therefore best studied in their role as military commanders, in the original connotation as *bey*s of *sancak*s, i.e., "commands."

One aspect of the military character of the *dirlik* system was that the *dirlik* was meant not only for the holder's own livelihood, but also for support of retinues of each *dirlik* holder. The smallest standard *timar* was the amount sufficient for the holder to maintain his horse and his arms and to allow him to join campaigns paying all his own expenses. If a *dirlik* holder was granted double this minimum, he was required to maintain and bring to campaigns an additional fully-armed horseman, called a *cebelü*. Around 1500 this standard minimum seems to have been about 3,000 *akçe*s. For each additional 3,000 *akçe*s of income the *timar* holder maintained one more *cebelü* in his retinue. For holders of high *dirlik*s, the ratio was one *cebelü* per 5,000 *akçe*s of income.[28] *Dirlik* holders were also required to bring along on campaigns their own equipment in addition to horses, arms, and armor. The *timar* holder, if he had two or three men in his little household, brought his own tent. The *sancakbeyi*, depending on his income, might have fifty to one hundred men in his retinue, and his baggage would comprise several tents of various types and sizes, cooking utensils, and other equipment.[29] The *sancakbeyi*, then, was the commander of the *dirlik* holders and all their retinues.

Not only did the *sancakbeyi* lead the cavalry of his district to battle, but he was also a key figure in the functioning of the *dirlik* system. The position of the *sancakbeyi* as commander of the *dirlik* holders of his *sancak* is symbolized by the fact that the wedding dues (*resm-i arūsāne*) of the *timar* holder's daughters were paid to the governor.[30] This authority was exercised in the disciplining of the *dirlik* holders under him, either directly by the *sancakbeyi* or, upon his recommendation, by higher authorities.[31] The governor's recommendation was also necessary for the dismissal of a *dirlik* holder from his *timar*, as punishment for grave transgressions.[32]

In appendix 3, in the course of a discussion of the granting of and changes in a district governor's *hās*, we note that it was the *sancakbeyi* himself who reported to the *beylerbeyi*'s office vacant *timar*s that could be incorporated in his own holdings. In the case of some *timar*s the previous owner had died; in other cases, however, the *sancakbeyi* cited dereliction of duty on the part of the *timar* holder as cause of dismissal. (See appendix 3, Synopsis and Comments.) On the same facsimiles from the *dirlik*-grant register there are further examples, instructive but not transliterated, because they did not constitute part of the governor's *hās*. On f. 627b there are three entries of *timar* assignments. The first entry records a *timar* granted to Mehmed bin Hacı, previously held by Celāl, with the explanation that the *sancakbeyi* first reported that Celāl was deceased, and second that Mehmed was indeed a son (*sahih çelebi oğlu*) of Hacı, a deceased *timar* holder, therefore deserving a *timar* himself. The *sancakbeyi* is here shown making recommendations both for dismissal and for granting. The other entries, however, indicate that other officials also played a role in the *timar*-granting process, at least in special circumstances. In the second entry, again on f. 627b, we learn that Nasuh bin Hasan Subaşı was dismissed from his *timar*, on 26 Şevval 948, on the *sancakbeyi*'s report that he "went home on the pretext of replenishing his funds" (*harçlık bahanesiyle evine gidüb . . .*) five months earlier and had not attended the defense of Buda. The last entry on the same page, however, records that this Nasuh bin Hasan Subaşı was granted a *timar* with equivalent yield but in another district a month later, on 28 Zilkade 948, upon bringing a report from the *kadı* of his subdistrict (*kadısından arz getirüb . . .*) attesting that Nasuh had been ill and confined to bed for a long time (*hayli zamandan marīz ve sāhib-i firāş olub . . .*), but that he was well again and ready for imperial service (*hāliyā ifakat bulub girü hidemāt-ı pādişāhiye geldüğin . . .*). Here it is a magistrate who is instrumental in the reinstitution of a dismissed *timar* holder. The crucial difference between the role of the *sancakbeyi* and that of the *kadı* should be noted. While a *sancakbeyi*, as an officer of the provincial cavalry, recommended dismissal or bestowal, the *kadı* merely reported the facts in his capacity as magistrate, as he might have done in any other matter, civil, commercial, or criminal.

Finally, f. 710a contains two rather special examples. Here, the persons granted *timar*s happened to be close to the governor general of the province, Bāli Paşa, in whose name the *dirlik*-grant register was kept and the appointment certificates (*tezkere*), subject to the sultan's approval, were issued. The first, Mustafa bin Kemal, was a relative (*hiyş, akraba*) of the *beylerbeyi*, and the second, Ayas Voyvoda, a member of his household (*merdüm, adam*). In these examples, special as they are, there is no mention of a *sancakbeyi* recommendation; the *beylerbeyi* made the grants directly. That the district governor was bypassed in these cases, however, seem to have been an exception due to the special circumstances of the persons involved.

The *sancakbeyi*, then, was the immediate supervisor of the provincial cavalry. He was assisted in this job by an *alaybeyi*, troop leader, and by the *subaşı*s, commanders of the subdistricts. In times of campaigns, the troops of the district collected under his banner, his *sancak* in the original connotation. In battle the sultan or the field commander sometimes gave a *sancak* specific duties; a *sancak*, therefore, was a discreet unit capable of performing particular tasks. Nevertheless, the usual order of battle for *sancak*s of a province was to march together under the command of the *beylerbeyi*. We have, then, to consider the authority of the governor general in order to place the *sancakbeyi* in proper perspective.

The *Beylerbeyi* and the Province

In the fourteenth century the *sancak* was the only territorial division in Ottoman lands and the *beylerbeyi*, at the time the office first emerged, was the commander-in-chief of all provincial troops. By the end of the century two other *beylerbeyi* came into being and the office was territorialized. In the 1460s a fourth *beylerbeyi* was created and as late as the beginning of the sixteenth century only four *beylerbeyi* were in command of the provinces of Rumeli (Balkan districts), Anadolu (west and north-central Anatolia districts), Rum (northeastern Anatolia districts), and Karaman (central and southern Anatolia districts). Then, as a result of vast territorial conquests from the 1510s through the 1530s the number of provinces rose to about fifteen. During this time the *sancak* remained the principle administrative unit and state regulations, dealing both with the *reāyā* and the provincial cavalry, underscored this position. *Kānūnnāme*s and cadastral surveys were prepared for each district, in recognition of the significance of regional variations in geography and customs.[33] More specifically, in dealing with the subjects, the criminal code required that a culprit be tried and punished in the district where the crime had been committed.[34] In terms of the *dirlik* system, too, the integrity of the district was emphasized, not only by requiring *timar* holders to reside in the district where their *timar* was located, but also by stipulating that vacant *timar*s in a district be granted only to cavalrymen who had previously held *timar*s there.[35]

The province, then, was a collection of districts, and the governor general was the commander of all the district governors. But in effect the governor general, too, was a *sancakbeyi*, inasmuch as the chief district of the province was his own preserve. The fairly sharp distinctions among lower ranks did not quite obtain between the *sancakbeyi* and the *beylerbeyi* ranks. In terms of pay, for example, the lowest grade *subaşı* received about ten times the yield of the smallest *timar*, and the most inexperienced *sancakbeyi* held ten times the revenues of the smallest *zeāmet*. On the other hand, the difference between the lowest *sancak hās*, 150,000–200,000 *akçe*s, and the lowest *beylerbeyi hās*, 600,000 *akçe*s was only about fourfold. The income of an experienced *sancakbeyi* could exceed 500,000 *akçe*s while the highest ranking *beylerbeyi* did not receive much beyond a million *akçe*s. The distinction in title, too, between *bey* and *paşa*, was not yet clearly established in the early sixteenth century, when many *beylerbeyi* still held the rank of *bey* (see appendix 1, section B).

The authority of the *beylerbeyi* over the province manifested itself primarily in terms of military organization.[36] In battle the troops of a province usually marched together under the *beylerbeyi*'s command. In terms of the operation of the *dirlik* system, some of the sultan's prerogatives were delegated to the governor general. In addition to records and registers kept in Istanbul in the imperial palace, each *beylerbeyi* kept copies of the *dirlik* registers and also a *dirlik* grant register where changes in titles to *dirlik*s were entered.[37]

At each provincial seat two officials, both of *zaim* rank, assisted the *beylerbeyi* in the supervision of *dirlik* grants, one a *timar defterdarı*, intendant of *timar* registers, and the other *timar* (sometimes *defter*) *kethüdası*, steward of the *zeāmet* holders. The *beylerbeyi* had the authority to effect *timar* grants, usually on the recommendation of the *sancakbeyi*, and issue appointment certificates (*tezkere*), which were sent to Istanbul for approval and issuance of the imperial diploma of office (*berāt-ı humāyūn*). Again, upon the recommendation of the *sancakbeyis*, the *beylerbeyi* dismissed *timar* holders deserving of punishment, subject to the sultan's approval. Furthermore, the *beylerbeyi* could grant small *timars* on his own authority without notifying the central government.[38] Higher *dirlik* grants, however, certainly all *sancakbeyi* appointments, were made directly by the sultan.

Inasmuch as there were revenues in each province, though not necessarily in each district of a province, reserved for the sultan (*havāss-ı humāyūn*), there was another official, also of *zaim* rank, in each provincial capital, called *hazīne* (sometimes *māl*) *defterdarı*, in charge of such revenues. Although the *dirlik* officials mentioned above, as well as the *hazīne defterdarı*, were appointed by the sultan and were not members of the *beylerbeyi*'s personal retinue, the *hazīne defterdarı* was even more independent of the *beylerbeyi* since he was not involved in the *dirlik* system. All these officials, with the addition of the *kadı* of the provincial capital, sat under the *beylerbeyi* in the provincial council (*divān*), a replica of the imperial council in Istanbul.

Both in the center and in the provinces, then, the highest authority was entrusted to the representatives of the military-administrative tradition, the grand vezir and the *beylerbeyi* respectively. Separate departments and traditions of administration were represented in both the imperial and the provincial council. In the imperial council sat the *nişancı*, head of the chancery and specialist in sultanic laws and regulations and the *defterdār*, high treasurer, representing the two branches of the bureaucracy, in addition to the two *kadıaskers*, heads of the legal-administrative system. The corresponding representatives on the provincial council were the *timar defterdarı*, the *timar kethüdası*, the *hazīne defterdarı*, and the *kadı*.

All these officials rose within their own departments and traditions and were directly appointed by the sultan; nevertheless the military-administrative officers were ascendant, they "chaired" the meetings, so to speak. If the exact authority of the grand vezir and of the *beylerbeyi* over the other bureaus was somewhat ambiguous, this was deliberate, for ultimately all authority was in the hands of the sultan.

CHAPTER 3

The Ümerā *Status*

EVER SINCE MACHIAVELLI cited the Ottoman empire as the prime example of a government "by a prince and his servants," in modern terms a bureaucratic empire, as opposed to a government "by a prince and by barons," a feudal state exemplified by the France of his day, European political commentators have been intrigued by the structure of the Ottoman state, so different from anything known in their own political traditions.[1] In Machiavelli's comments on the Ottoman system there is neither praise nor derogation: he merely wishes to distinguish between the two types of state to show that while the first would be difficult to conquer, but easy to hold once conquered, the opposite would be true in the case of the feudal state, easier to conquer but more difficult to control. The key difference, according to Machiavelli, is in the personnel of the state: in the Ottoman empire the officers are "all slaves, and dependent" on the sultan; the French king, on the other hand, "is surrounded by a large number of ancient nobles." A few generations later Ogier Ghiselin de Busbecq, twice ambassador of Charles V to the court of Suleiman the Magnificient, thus a first-hand observer of the Ottoman state, made a similar distinction, but in a different context, between the European rulers, dependent on their nobility, and the Ottoman sultan, master of his slaves in public offices. Busbecq commented that the lack of a blood-nobility in the system allowed the sultan to pick his slaves and advance them according to their abilities; the system was a meritocracy where there was no impediment to the rise of any man to the highest offices other than his own capacity.[2] The shepherd who rose to become an illustrious grand vezir was a figure that never ceased to fascinate European observers.

What in the Ottoman empire surprised the Renaissance observers was actually a feature which had long been established in Islamic near-eastern states. The extensive use of specially trained slaves, *mamluks*, for military-administrative purposes had started during the Abbasid empire in Baghdad in the ninth century; from that time most, if not all, Islamic states had a similar institution; on at least two occasions, in the thirteenth century in Egypt and in India, the *mamluks* established states of their own where even the sultan was chosen from their ranks.[3] Slaves to be trained as administrators had to be non-Muslims, for a Muslim could not become a slave (although a slave could, and was normally expected to, become a Muslim and remain a slave). Nor could the non-Muslim inhabitants of a Muslim state be taken as slaves, for they had a definite legal status as *zimmîs*, certainly not equal to Muslim citizens, but nevertheless one which accorded them certain rights and guarantees, including personal freedom. The traditional source of slaves of the state was, therefore, outside Islamic lands: prisoners of war from among non-Muslim enemies, slaves sold at the slave market, or presented by friendly or vassal rulers. The Ottomans, from around 1400, started to levy children from their own non-Muslim subjects: this practice did not agree with established customs of Islamic states or with Islamic law, but the Ottomans did it and were not challenged on legal grounds. The practice, called *devşirme*, of levying children within Ottoman lands had an advantage over other sources of slaves in that it afforded a considerable degree of selection in recruitment for the system. It probably explains why, even though the *devşirme* supplied only about a third of the total number of slaves introduced into the Ottoman system, most slaves who rose highest in the ranks were of *devşirme* origin.[4]

The purpose of the *mamluk* institution was, of course, precisely to avoid the development of a blood-nobility and to maintain a hand-picked, well-trained group of officials absolutely loyal to the ruler. Their loyalty would be assured because, theoretically, the *mamluk*s, cut off from their roots, were left with no ties but to their master. In reality the *mamluk*s did develop ties among themselves, based upon common experiences after they became slaves, or on shared or similar ethnic and regional backgrounds; nor were they ever completely cut off from their original homelands.[5] Furthermore, contemporary European observers, in their enthusiasm for the distinctive and different aspects of the Ottoman system, overlooked one of its major features; namely that slaves were by no means the only source of manpower for the Ottoman military-administrative establishment.

Although it never reached the proportions of a true blood-nobility, the Ottoman system allowed the sons and other relatives of the servant-officials of the sultan, whether they themselves had been slaves or free-born, to enter into its ranks. This was done chiefly by granting the sons of officials some official status in provincial administration the level of which depended on the father's rank, among other things. Also, more importantly, a very small number of sons and brothers of the highest officials were placed in a special corps, called the *müteferrika*, in the palace outside service (*bīrūn*). Thus, in palace service, slaves and the sons of the most prominent Ottomans were brought together. As for the military-administrative system as a whole, there were slaves, sons of slaves, descendants of slaves, and descendants of families of Turkish origin or families which had been Turkified, working side by side.

Halil İnalcık, the master of Ottoman studies, has traced the career lines of slaves entering the Ottoman system in a table which perceptively summarizes also the relationship of palace service and provincial administration in the "classical" period, i.e., the sixteenth century.[6] İnalcık's purpose was to show only how the *slaves* advanced. An expanded picture is presented here in chart 3.1, based upon İnalcık's table but including more points of entry into the system. It is, at the same time, more stream-lined, with some details omitted so that the essential points are highlighted. (Chart 3.1 also incorporates the relevant findings of my present research for the period 1568–1574; the findings for the period 1630–1640 will be presented in a similar chart, 4.1.)

There were four possible ways of becoming a member of the

CHART 3.1 MILITARY-ADMINISTRATIVE CAREER LINES
IN THE MID-SIXTEENTH CENTURY

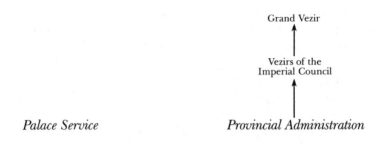

Central Administration

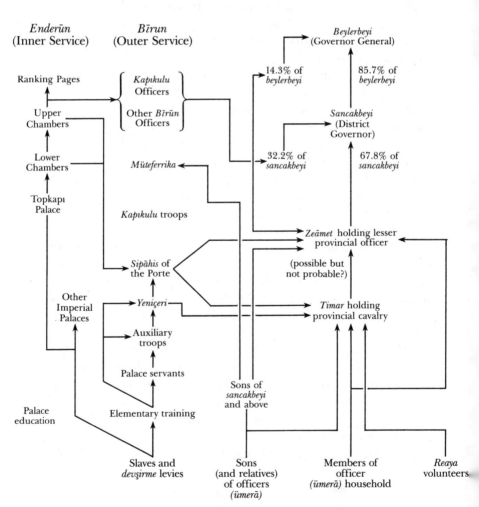

Palace Service   *Provincial Administration*

military-administrative establishment: as a *reāyā* volunteer, a
descendent of those already in the system, a member of officers'
households, and as a slave. The relative importance of these channels changed considerably in the course of the sixteenth and seventeenth centuries. In the early days, when the state institutions were
relatively unstructured, many volunteers who joined the frontier
raiders (*ghazi*, later *akıncı*) were granted *timar*s in return for their
services. They settled down in what became interior areas as the
frontier moved farther into enemy territory. It was recognized that
their sons should receive priority in the granting of new *timar*s, but
so long as there were new conquests and therefore new areas where
*timar*s could be created and distributed, there does not seem to have
been competition between the sons of *timar* holders and new *reāyā*
volunteers. In the late fifteenth and early sixteenth centuries,
however, presumably because even the successful campaigns on
the European frontiers resulted not so much in new conquests as in
extending Ottoman power over areas which retained internal
autonomy, new *timar*s became scarcer and frictions did develop. In
the early reign of Süleyman I, in the 1520s, *timar* holders, to secure
a place for their offspring, demanded that new candidates, volunteers not related to *timar* holders, be disregarded completely, claim-
ing they were "foreigners" (*ecnebi!*), i.e., presumably "foreign" to
the system. It seems also that it was during this time that a rigid
view of society began to develop which proclaimed that sons of
reāyā should remain *reāyā* and not enter the military-administrative
class. Writing his reflections on the business of government after his
retirement in 1541, Lütfi Paşa, a grand vezir of Süleyman's reign,
observed that the ruler or his vezirs should be resolute in keeping
the *reāyā* out of *timar*-holder ranks.[7] The fear was that if all the *reāyā*
joined the campaigns, aspiring to become *timar* holders, nobody
would be left to till the land and pay the taxes.

In an edict issued in 1531, Süleyman addressed himself to this
problem: "Those living in my domains, either officers or subjects,
all of them are my servants. How can the people of my own land
and realm be called 'foreigners'!" the sultan asked ("*İmdi, benim
memālik-i mahrūsemde vāki olan eğer sipahilerdir ve eğer reāyādır, cümlesi
kullarımdır; kendü memleketim ve vilāyetim halkı nice ecnebi olur*"). He

TABLE 3.1. Annual Income of Offices to be Given to Sons of *Ümerā* (figures in *akçes*)

Fathers (*rank and official income*)		Province Governor (Beylerbeyi)		District Governor (Sancakbeyi)			
		Rumeli and Anadolu	*Others*	700,000	500,000–700,000	300,000–500,000	100,000–300,000
Sons							
Already *dirlik* holding		Annual income will be brought in line with the rates given below; if sons already hold *dirliks* equal to or above these rates, they will be given raises of 6,000, 5,000, or 4,000.					
Sons of age	1 son	40,000	35,000	30,000	25,000	20,000	15,000
	2 sons	25,000	20,000	—	—	20,000	15,000
	3 or more sons	45,000 to be divided among them	35,000 to be divided among them	15,000 11,000 11,000	10,000 9,000 9,000	—	8,000 6,000 6,000
1 minor son		—	—	—	12,500	10,000	—

TABLE 3.2 Size of *Tīmars* to be Given to Sons of *Ẕeāmet* or *Tīmar* Holders

Fathers (rank and official income)		Lesser Provincial Officer (Subāṣı-Zaīm)				Tīmar Holder			
		Fallen in battle		*Natural death*		*Fallen in battle*		*Natural death*	
Sons		50,000– 100,000	20,000– 50,000	50,000– 100,000	20,000– 50,000	10,000– 20,000	under 10,000	10,000– 20,000	under 10,000
Already *Tīmar* holding (raise)	First	3000	2000	—	—	—	—	—	—
	Second	2000	1500	—	—	—	—	—	—
Sons of adult age	First	8000	6000	6000	5000	4000	3000	3000	2000
	Second	6000	5000	5000	4000	3000	2000	2000	2000
	Third	—	4000	—	—	—	—	—	—
	Others	should serve in campaigns to deserve *timar*		—	—	—	—	—	—
Sons: minors	1 son	3000	2500	2500	2000	2000	2000	should serve in campaigns to deserve *timar*	
	2 sons	6000*	5000*	5000*	4000*	3000*	3000*		

*Held jointly.

recognized the *reāyā*-turned-*timar*-holders and restored their offices to those among them who had recently had their *dirlik*s taken away just because they were not related to *timar* holders.[8] But from then on it appears that *reāyā* volunteers had to serve provincial officers, *beylerbeyi* and *sancakbeyi* especially, more directly, if they were to have any hope of being nominated by them for consideration in the granting of *timar*s. In the late sixteenth century, after successful campaigns, provincial officers submitted lists of their candidates for *timar* grants;[9] the way for a *reāyā* volunteer to become a *timar* holder was to pass through service in the household of an officer. There had always been retainers or slaves of *ümerā* who were granted *timar*s, so that service in a household had traditionally been a point of entry into the system, but as there came to be more restrictions on new candidates, the importance of service to high-level officials increased, not only for *reāyā* volunteers but even for sons of *timar* holders.

In the same edict, Süleyman also issued regulations, sum-marized in Tables 3.1 and 3.2 governing the granting of *dirlik*s to the sons of *dirlik* holders.[10] The major determinant of the size of the *timar* a son received on his father's death was, as might be expected, the rank of his father. How the father died, i.e., whether on campaign or of natural causes, how many sons he left behind, and whether the sons were of age to take part in campaigns were other considerations. The manner of the father's death was a factor only for the sons of minor officers, an incentive to participate in cam-paigns and to fight well. The *ümerā* obviously did not need to be killed in battle to prove their worth. There was no question of passing on to sons their father's positions; the sons were given offices with incomes only a fraction (roughly 5–10 percent) of what the father had enjoyed, nor had the *dirlik* given the sons any geograph-ical connection with the positions held by the fathers. Nevertheless, the principle was that sons of Ottoman officers, if they chose, should be given a place in the military-administrative structure proportionate to their father's rank after their father died. The sons of higher level officials were sometimes given *dirlik*s during their father's lifetime; in such cases the *dirlik*-holding sons were given raises upon the father's death.

A very small number of sons of *ümerā* entered their father's career, not in the provincial administration as was usual, but in palace service, as *müteferrika*s. The *müteferrika* were a special corps in the outside service (*bīrūn*); the term literally means "various" and reflected the fact that the *müteferrika* included several kinds of officers.[11] In a register of monthly payments to *bīrūn* officers dated 942–43 (1535–37), for example, three different groups of *müteferrika* are specified: those who perform special services to the sultan, five persons; the sons and brothers of vezirs and other officers, thirty-six persons; and other *müteferrika*, mostly people retired from active service in various palace or government posts, twenty-two persons.[12] Many of the persons cited in the second group are members of the Ottoman imperial family, sons of vassal rulers, e.g., the Crimean Han and some Kurdish *beys*, and sons of deposed rulers of conquered lands, e.g., Mamluk Egypt and the Dulkadir state. A majority, however, seem to be the sons of Ottoman officers. Lütfi Paşa, the grand vezir, comments that only persons from the inner service (*enderūn*) and the sons of *beylerbeyi* and high financial officers should be allowed into the *müteferrika* corps.[13] However, the number of sons of Ottoman officials who actually became *müteferrika*s of the imperial palace was relatively so small that this group seems to have been the exception to prove the rule that only slaves served in the palace. The purpose of this exception must have been to allow at least *some ümerā* sons to experience the palace atmosphere. How the handful of *ümerā* sons to be admitted into palace service was chosen is not clear. It should be added that one sometimes comes across *ümerā* relatives elsewhere in the *bīrūn*. In the 1530s two of the highest *bīrūn* officers were *ümerā* relatives; whether or not they had earlier been among the *müteferrika*, is not known.[14] Finally, it should be emphasized that the mechanisms which favored *ümerā* sons did not lead to the formation of an Ottoman "aristocracy." The sons started their careers at a much lower level than the ranks their fathers had attained and, more importantly, they still owed their positions to the will of the sultan.

Not only the sons of officers but also their retainers, whether free-born or of slave origin, could enter the military-administrative career. There were highly exceptional cases of *ümerā* retainers among the *müteferrika*,[15] but for members of *ümerā* households the usual channel of entry into the military-administrative career in state service was through provincial administration. One of Süleyman's *fermans* regulating *timar* grants specified that upon the death of a *paşa* twelve officers of his household were to be given *timars* of various sizes.[16] But already during the lifetime of their masters many *ümerā* retainers received *dirliks* from the state. In a register of *dirliks* (*icmāl defteri*) of Hersek district dated 904/1498–99 it is entered that in all thirty-five *dirliks* were held by the relatives and retainers of twenty-one officers of various ranks.[17] Apparently at least some of the officers were still alive when the register was drawn up. More definite examples are provided by a Rumeli *dirlik*-grant register (*rūzname*) from the years 948–49/1541–42: in these years in various parts of the general region of Rumeli (the European territories of the empire) Rüstem Paşa's retainers, for example, held three *zeāmets* and seven *timars*; those of Ahmed Paşa, the governor of Rumeli province, held two *zeāmets* and seventeen *timars*; Hüsrev Paşa's men held three *zeāmets* and seventeen *timars*.[18] All three *paşas* were alive at the time. There is even the case of Murad Gâzi who was appointed *sancakbeyi* of Klis when he was the *kethüdā* (chief household officer) of Hüsrev Bey, the *sancakbeyi* of Bosna, as reward for the *kethüdā*'s services on the Bosnian frontier.[19] At that time, in the 1530s, it seems to have been exceptional to join the provincial administration directly from a private household at such a high level, without having held any previous state appointment. Presumably it was owing to the exceptional circumstances of the frontier zone that such an appointment took place. We shall later see that during the period under study members of *ümerā* households came to hold a much higher percentage of total *dirliks* and that they joined provincial administration at higher ranks.

The last and, along with the sons of *ümerā*, the most important avenue of entry into the military-administrative career was through the largest household—the sultan's own. Since, with the exception of the *müteferrika*, only slaves could enter the palace organization, and since palace training gave one a great advantage at the start of a career in the military-administrative system, many observers of the Ottoman empire presumed that *only* the sultan's slaves occupied the high echelons of the system. There may be other explanations for modern historians making the same— mistaken—assumption. One is that, although people of various origins served in most ranks of the military-administrative structure, the highest office of all, the grand vezirate, was left almost exclusively to the sultan's slaves after the mid-fifteenth century. Officers of other than slave origin continued to rise, even to become vezirs of the imperial council, but there they stopped—as if by an unwritten and unspoken rule that only real (and imperial) slaves could become grand vezir. This fact, I think, more than anything else, caused many students of Ottoman history to assume that the slaves took over *all* the more important offices.

A second explanation for this assumption may be due to the ambiguity of the term *kul*, the most widely used, though not the only, Ottoman word for "slave" reared for an official career (others are: *gulâm*, pl. *gilmân*; *bende*; *iç oğlanı*). Ménage has commented on this ambiguity and established that, in addition to its primary and specific meaning of "slave," "*kul*" was also used in a more general manner to mean something like "servant."[20] To make the point Ménage quoted (among other things) an exchange between the Duke of Savoy and an Ottoman official sent to Europe on a special mission in the 1480s.[21]

Here is this highly instructive exchange (in Ménage's translation): "'What is your status? Are you a *kul* of the sultan?' asks the duke. 'I am.' 'What is your descent?' 'I am Turkish born.' 'One who is Turkish-born cannot be the sultan's *kul*.' 'Your excellency is right, but I am the son of a *kul*; I eat the Sultan's bread and so count as his *kul*.'" The rest of the exchange, which Ménage omits, is also relevant. The duke asks further: "How am I to know that you are the sultan's *kul*? You don't have a document from the sultan." The Ottoman officer answers that the sultan (the term he uses is *hünkâr*) is now far away, but that he could get a document (*hüccet*) from the Genoese corroborating that he is a *kul* of the sultan. The official, Barak Reis, claims he is a *kul* not necessarily because his father was a genuine *kul* but because he himself "eats the sultan's bread," i.e., works for him and receives pay. In this sense any Ottoman official, of whatever origin, could be termed "*kul*." Also, when the duke asks for the sultan's signet, he is interested not so much in determining that Barak Reis is a *slave* as that he is a genuine Ottoman official, the sultan's *servant*. There is yet a third sense of *kul*, obviously current in the first half of the sixteenth century, attested in the sultan's own words. In his *ferman* regulating *timar* grants, Sultan Süleyman called both *timar* holders and the *reāyā* subjects, his *kul*. This usage is even broader than the second; here "*kullarım*" is as nondescript as "my people." Given such varied levels of meanings, one should beware of assuming that when an Ottoman is called a "*kul*" in the sources he is necessarily a slave.

That officers not of slave origin continued to play an important role in the sixteenth century is supported by the information summarized in table 3.3. The table is based on lists prepared to show at a given time which officer held which *sancak* with what revenues.[22] The officers are identified, if at all, either by immediately preceding post, invariably in the palace outside (*bīrūn*) service or as relatives of other officers. The table reflects this feature of the lists. However, these two categories are not strictly speaking mutually exclusive; we have seen that *ümerā* relatives could also become palace officials, as *müteferrika* or in some other category. They may have been *sancakbeyi*, who could have been mentioned in both categories. If so, the official who drew up the list must have decided that one category was more important and the hypothetical *ümerā*-related palace official was mentioned only in that more important category. We may also assume that the "unidentified" group was made up of people excluded from both categories, i.e., were probably lesser provincial officers not related to *ümerā* but who may have been palace officials shifted to provincial administration at a lower rank, in other words whose *immediately* preceding post was not in palace service. Based on this assumption, this group could also be termed "various." (Less likely, it may have been that the official who prepared the list simply neglected to enter the palace office or the *ümerā* connection of some of these in the "unidentified" group; if so this category should be disregarded altogether in the interpretation of the table.)

It is remarkable that the *ümerā*-related group comprises such a large portion (40.5 and 42.7 percent) of the total number of

TABLE 3.3. District Governors (*Sancakbeyi*) in the 1520s.

Sancakbeyi	I. Ümerā Related		II. Kapıkulu & Other Birun Officers		III. Unidentified (various?)		TOTAL	
	1521	*1527*	*1521*	*1527*	*1521*	*1527*	*1521*	*1527*
Provinces								
Rumeli	16	14	7	6	9	8	32	28
Anadolu	4	7	7	4	5	4	16	15
Karaman	3	—	2	3	2	2	7	5
Rum	—	5	3	—	1	6	4	11
Arab (1521)	6		4		4		14	
Şam (1527)		7		1		6		14
Mısr (1527)		—		—		2		2
Diyarbekir	3	2	1	—	2	5	6	7
TOTAL	32	35	24	14	23	33	79	82
Percent	40.5	42.7	30.4	17.1	29.1	40.2	100.0	100.0

SOURCE: TSA, D.9772 and TSA, D.5246.

Notes:

1. Table excludes *beylerbeyi* (province governors), *yaya*, and *müsellem* commanders in Anadolu province, and Kurdish tribal chiefs.

2. Persons identified by family name, e.g., "Aranid oğlu" and "Mihaloğlu," are included in the first category.

3. Number of *sancaks* here does not add up to total number of *sancaks* in the empire as some *sancaks* were vacant or had been turned into *hās* or *arpalık* (*tekaüdlük* here) at the time the lists were prepared.

4. "Arab" province had been divided into Şam (Syria) and Mısr (Egypt) provinces by 1527.

5. See Appendix I for more information on the lists; the text, transcription, and translation of TSA, D.5246 is given there.

sancakbeyis; what is perhaps even more remarkable is that they are more numerous than *sancakbeyi* appointed directly from *bīrūn* posts.[23] Together both groups were the *kuls* of the sultan, his servant officers; the fact that some of them were of genuine slave origin (*gulām*) while others were freeborn of Turkish fathers or were of Turkish origin seems to have had scant significance, legally or socially. It seems unlikely that there would have been a rivalry between the "Turkish aristocracy" so to speak and the slaves, as some historians have claimed, because the sons of slaves could join that "aristocracy."

Social Standing

In general terms we can determine who the *ümerā* were, that is, from what social background they came, as a group if not individually. Some aspects of the professional career of the *ümerā*, too, can be ascertained and are discussed in part in chapters 2 and 4. It is much more difficult to answer questions about the various stages of their personal lives before they attained *ümerā* ranks, questions concerning education and marriage patterns, for example. Neither is there sufficient information on nonprofessional activities, such as cultural interests or business ventures. There are even questions concerning the *ümerā*'s professional lives which remain unanswered, such as how a household is formed and how it functions. The evidence on which answers may be based is scanty; it is certainly not of a nature to allow the kind of systematic treatment that is attempted in the following chapter on the structure of the *ümerā* career. The discussion of the social standing of the *ümerā* is, therefore, bound to be impressionistic; more holes and gaps in information will be pointed out than solid footing can be provided.

The four sources of manpower for the military-administrative career enumerated above can be reduced to two in terms of preparation for the *ümerā* ranks. The *reāyā* volunteers are left out of the discussion, since it was extremely unlikely that such persons could cross the barrier between the *timar* rank and *zaīm* status. Even when they succeeded in getting *timar* grants, which was becoming extremely difficult in the sixteenth century, they could not hope to reach higher ranks in the *dirlik* system. As for persons joining *ümerā* households as a first step in advancement, they may be considered, for our present purposes, together with *ümerā* sons. We will take up the households, then, those of the sultan, the imperial palace, on one hand, and of the *ümerā* themselves, on the other, as main channels of recruitment and preparation.

Relatively more information exists on the functioning of the imperial household, although even here there is room for considerable revision in views generally accepted at present. It is known, for example, that in addition to the *devşirme* and to slaves acquired in other ways, the slaves of a deceased official were sometimes admitted into the imperial palace.[24] But since not much is known about "private" households, the implications of such admittance have not been recognized. Lists of slaves in private households in the mid-sixteenth century have recently come to light and some have been published.[25] All such lists, however, concern the households of men who held the same office, *bāb üs-saāde ağası*, the chief white eunuch, who was the most powerful official of the imperial palace in this period and the only palace official who was officially allowed to maintain a household outside the palace.[26] Although the *bāb üs-saāde ağası* was a highly exceptional case and the lists cannot be used as instances of a general phenomenon, nevertheless some features of these households need to be noted.

One puzzling fact is that some private household slaves appear to have volunteered for the position. In a list where not only the provenance but also the method of acquisition of each "slave" is noted, ten out of 122 are said to have "become slaves of their own volition" (*iradesiyle bende olmuştur*).[27] The indication is that not only the term *kul* but the slave status itself was highly ambiguous, at least by the sixteenth century. Such volunteers must have been subjects of the empire, for it is difficult to imagine foreigners coming to seek employment, so to speak, in an Ottoman household. Attaching oneself to the household of an Ottoman official, even in the ambiguous status of a "slave," must have been an acceptable way of social advancement.

A second observation concerns Cafer Ağa, a *bāb üs-saāde ağası* himself. Two of his "slaves" are noted as having been slaves of his own previous master, that is, his master before Cafer Ağa became a servant of the sultan.[28] When Cafer Ağa entered the imperial palace, presumably on his previous master's death, these two other slaves of the master remained with Cafer Ağa, as *his* "slaves," or simply as members of his household. The problem, which may not be readily apparent, is this: supposing that Cafer Ağa was taken into the imperial palace upon his previous master's death, why did not the other two also become the sultan's slaves? Further, presumably Cafer Ağa entered the sultan's service not as *bāb üs-saāde ağası* but at a lower rank; in that case, since he was not allowed to maintain an outside household until he became *bāb üs-saāde ağası*, how and where did he keep those two as his slaves? The same list indicates that some of Cafer Ağa's slaves, other than the two discussed here, were already in the imperial palace, although they were serving Cafer Ağa and not the sultan directly.[29] Perhaps, then, before Cafer Ağa was allowed to furnish an outside household, before he rose to become *bāb üs-saāde ağası*, he already had his own retinue in the palace. Admittedly this is speculative, but the conclusion, given these indications, is that palace officials in the sixteenth century had their own little "households" in the palace, not composed solely of the sultan's slaves. Judging by the lists, such "households" within the sultan's household seem to have been recognized and were not just informal groupings.

This finding is important for it provides a clue as to how officials formed their households once they left the palace to take up positions either in central government or in provincial administration. Setting out from the palace was not an individual affair. The transfer of pages from the inner service (*enderūn*) to the outer (*bīrūn*), or of the *bīrūn* officers to government posts took place at fixed intervals, every few years, and involved most members of the palace organization.[30] In the process, called *çıkma*, literally "setting out," some pages were promoted to higher positions in the *enderūn* while some were sent out to the *bīrūn* or to serve as *timar*-holding cavalry in the provinces; *bīrūn* officers received higher positions in the *dirlik* system (see chart 3.1). We have seen that from the *timar* holders up, all officials were required to maintain households the size of which was commensurate with rank and revenues received. If some higher-ranking palace officials did indeed have their own retinues inside the palace, such a retinue would serve as the nucleus of the household that the official needed to set up once outside the palace. Also there are indications that lower-level "graduates" of the palace system joined households of higher-ranking officials sent out at the same *çıkma*, although this has been documented only for the seventeenth century.[31] How it was decided which junior officer joined the retinue of which senior one when hundreds of persons left the palace all at once is not clear. Friendships formed in the palace may have played a role.[32]

Connections were possible, then, between private households and the imperial household, both in how one gained entry to the palace at one end and, at the other, how one left it. The imperial palace provided its graduates not only with the beginnings of a household but, sometimes, with a family as well: girls who were educated and trained in the harem in various arts and crafts left the palace as wives of "graduating" pages.[33]

During his years in the *enderūn* a page was given a well-rounded education and training. All pages shared a basic education, which included Islamic and Ottoman classics in poetry, history, and belles-lettres. All pages also received training in military skills: horsemanship and the use of various weapons. Beyond this common education, pages followed their individual bents. Some excelled in horsemanship or skills in weaponry. Others pursued literary and artistic studies further. Some of the latter did not join the *dirlik* system at all but became scribes in the central chancery and the financial bureaus. Some literary-minded pages became scholars, historians, or even religious-legal experts. Some became artists, painters, musicians, and poets. In addition to those who gained repute as poets while also holding administrative jobs, many of the *ümerā* wrote poetry and are represented in biographical dictionaries of poets in large numbers.

Unfortunately we do not possess similar information on persons who were trained in other households. It would be a fairly safe guess, however, that the son of a *bey* or a *paşa* received a similar

gentleman's education. There certainly is no indication in Ottoman sources that there was any distinction between those trained
in the imperial palace and those raised in private households in
terms of values, level of education, and refinement, although individual differences undoubtedly obtained.

An example of the literary taste of a *sancakbeyi* is provided
in the estate left behind by a Yunus Bey who died in 1572.[34]
According to the list of thirty-two books in his estate, Yunus Bey
had catholic reading interests: books on Ottoman and Islamic
history, on jurisprudence and religion, literary works, and a
volume on chess were in his library. The collection was valued at
6,358 *akçe*s, with some collector's items fetching 1,000 *akçe*s each.
Yunus Bey's collection was smaller but much more valuable than
that of a college teacher (*müderris*).[35]

Another area in which satisfactory information is unavailable
is the length of time spent on education and training for the higher
ranks in provincial administration. We know that slaves admitted
into the imperial palace were about fifteen years of age on the
average and spent several years in the inner service. It may be
surmised that *ümerā* trained in the palace took up posts in the outer
service or as *timar* and *zeāmet* holders in their mid twenties. As for
sons of *ümerā*, we cannot even begin to guess how early they started
their careers.

There is one person, a Mehmed Bey, about whom some information has been recovered, but he seems to be an exception for he
was the son of a prominent vezir, Lala Mustafa Paşa. The specific
data on Mehmed Bey's career, established from the appointment
register MAD 563, are supplemented by the entry in *Sicill-i Osmāni*,
a late but comprehensive biographical dictionary. See appendix 4,
sample 5, Mehmed Bey/Paşa *veled-i* (son of) Mustafa Paşa.
Admittedly, the *Sicill-i Osmāni* is not a very accurate compilation;
in this particular case Mehmed Bey is said to have served as *beylerbeyi* of Musul, but the entries in the appointment register show that
this was not so.[36] Mehmed Bey is first mentioned in the appointment register as *sancakbeyi* of Safed (in Palestine), where he had
been transferred from Trablus (Tripoli in Lebanon). This was in
974/1566. After serving as *sancakbeyi* in Ankara and Niğde (in

central Anatolia), he was promoted to the rank of *beylerbeyi* in 979/1571 and received the title of *paşa*. His first post as *beylerbeyi* was at Maraş (Dulkadriye province in south-central Anatolia), a relatively unimportant province, in accordance with the fairly standard procedure by which a *bey* newly elevated to a higher rank was posted to a lesser district or province. A year later Mehmed Bey, now Paşa, was transferred to Halep (Aleppo), a much more important province. We learn from the *Sicill-i Osmāni* that Mehmed Paşa died two years later, in 982/1574, while still governor there. *Sicill-i Osmāni* notes that Mehmed Paşa was only thirty years old when he died. If this information is correct, Mehmed Bey was already a *sancakbeyi* at the age of twenty-two and attained the rank of *beylerbeyi* by the time he was twenty-seven. The young age of Mehmed Bey/Paşa when he held important offices, the speed with which he moved through the ranks, and the relatively high income he was granted even while he was a *sancakbeyi*, all seem to have been features of an exceptional career. He may have been a very capable commander; at the same time, however, he was the son of a vezir who was quite prominent at the time.

The career samples given in appendix 4 indicate different rates of progress for different governors. İbrahim Bey, for example (sample 1), first served in at least two *zeāmet*-level offices in Erzurum province. He was at such a post for three and a half years, and without appointment for three more years, before he was elevated in 978/1570 to *sancakbeyi* rank in a minor district with the minimum income for the rank (200,000 *akçes*). He held various posts for the next thirteen years, all third-rate *sancak*s, with scant increase in his revenues and for fairly lengthy periods without appointment. Sinan Bey (sample 2) seems to have had a more successful career as a northwestern frontier region specialist. He was consistently reappointed immediately after leaving each post except once when he had to wait five months. He also received a substantial raise in his income while he was governor of Arad (Timişvar province in southern Transylvania).

The next sample (no. 3) is Mustafa Bey, also the son of a vezir. Mustafa was among the rare *ümerā* sons who held an appointment at the imperial palace in the special *müteferrika* corps. His first post in provincial administration was as steward of the Aegean Islands province *timar* holders, the province of the commander of the navy. After serving at this post for more than two years, Mustafa Bey was elevated to *sancakbeyi* rank with an enormous revenue (350,000 *akçes*) for a new appointee. Again he might have been an exceptionally capable man, but we should note that at the time his father was second vezir (i.e., after the grand vezir) in Istanbul. His rapid rise may have been due to his father's influence, but he doesn't seem to have suffered from his father's disgrace after the debacle of Lepanto in the following year: he was left at his post undisturbed for three more years. The glory of the father may have reflected on the son's standing, but apparently the father's sin was not visited upon the son. The last two, Mehmed Bey (sample 4) and Ahmed Bey (sample 6), were both sons of paşas and had fairly successful careers, if not as spectacular as that of Mustafa Paşa's son Mehmed Bey. The fact that both went on to reach *beylerbeyi* rank appears to indicate that *ümerā* sons had an advantage over others.

The cases mentioned here are merely illustrations of more general findings discussed in the following chapter. The specific instances should be viewed against a background of trends established by aggregate analysis. Before we turn to study features of the *ümerā* career lines, however, there remains to discuss certain other aspects of the *ümerā* status in Ottoman polity, particularly the economic power of the *ümerā* and how it was passed on within the family.

While it is difficult to estimate the total revenues of members of the *ümerā* group, we can at least say that in the sixteenth century probably a major portion of the income of a *paşa* or *bey* accrued from his *hās*, the state revenues in the form of various taxes, dues, and fines allotted to him. There is some evidence in the Ottoman archives to support this view. According to a register showing the annual income and expenditures of Semiz Ali Paşa for the year 968/1560–61, while he was grand vezir, 2,577,918 *akçes*, or 73.1 percent of his total annual revenue of 3,529,139 *akçes*, were supplied by the *paşa's hās*.[37] In the case of an Erzurum *beylerbeyi*, unnamed in the register but probably to be identified as Ayas Paşa, in 962–63/1555–56, the share of the *hās* in total revenues was much higher: 2,138,183 out of 2,189,996 *akçe*s or 97.6 percent.[38] We lack similar documents for lower level officials such as the *sancakbeyi*, but it can be assumed that they were in a similar position. It can be further suggested that in their case the *hās* revenues constituted an even higher share of the total, since they were not as yet well-established enough to have extensive private earnings.

We have seen in our discussion of provincial administration (chapter 2) that the *sancakbeyi hās* started at a minimum of about 150,000 *akçe*s annually, although this minimum was raised to 200,000 *akçe*s in the second half of the sixteenth century. After some time at that rank, a *sancakbeyi* could hold an important *sancak* with revenues of up to 600,000 *akçe*s. The same level of income was granted to a new *beylerbeyi* at a minor province like Maraş, while a senior *beylerbeyi* could receive as much as two million *akçe*s, though this was rare. I have come across only a single case of a *sancakbeyi* granted 800,000 *akçe*s as annual income.[39] This enormous sum was given because the *bey* was appointed to an area newly conquered from the Mamluks in Cilicia in 1486 and he needed to maintain a large household to be able to defend the newly created district.[40] Leaving aside this exception, the official income of the *sancakbeyi* was between 200,000 and 600,000 *akçe*s, usually in the range of 250,000–400,000 *akçe*s.

The official *hās* assigned to a *bey* was not just personal income. He was required to maintain a group of retainers on the revenue assigned to him, was responsible for providing arms, armor, horses for the retainers, and for paying all their expenses on campaigns. Nevertheless, when one considers the estates left by *sancakbeyi*, especially in comparison with that of other segments of society, it is evident that the *ümerā* wielded considerable economic power.

As a first step in the consideration of the *ümerā*'s wealth an attempt must be made to establish how much money was "wealth" in sixteenth-century Ottoman society. The question, how many *akçe*s was a normal accumulation and how many *akçe*s constituted substantial wealth, difficult though they may be to answer, should nevertheless be posed. One guideline, however imperfect, is provided by the Ottoman method of classifying the subjects as poor, middle level, and well-to-do in levying some taxes and also in collecting some fines. For purposes of *cizye* (non-Muslim poll tax) collection, the ratio was one for the poor (*ednā, fakīr ül-hāl*), two for the middle level (*evsat, vasat ül-hāl*), and four for the well-to-do (*ālā, gani*). In terms of fines for various crimes and transgressions the rates changed, sometimes conforming to the 1 : 2 : 4 ratio as in the *cizye*, but sometimes closer to 1 : 2 : 3.[41] The first article of the criminal code, as published by Heyd, specifies what is meant by these categories.[42] According to this definition rich means "possessing one thousand *akçe* or more," middle level is having "property amounting to six hundred *akçe*," while a poor man has "property amounting to four hundred *akçe*." There is a fourth category here, not employed for tax purposes, that might be called the destitute, consisting of those in worse circumstances than the "official" poor. These figures are amazingly low. Even for subjects to consider possession of 1,000 *akçe*s as constituting wealth seems preposterous. Perhaps the problem is with Heyd's translation of the term "possession": in the original it reads "*akçeye kādir olsa, gücü yetse*," which may be translated more accurately, if in a more cumbersome way, as "being capable of [producing] so many *akçe*s" or, even more literally, as "affording so many *akçe*s." What is implied may be not total worth but cash holdings or liquid assets.

İnalcık has attempted to define economic status on the basis of estates entered in the court records of Bursa in the second half of the fifteenth century, concluding that a person was poor if his holdings did not exceed 20 ducats, about 1,000 *akçe*s, as in 26 percent of the cases he studied. Fifty-eight percent, with between 1,000 and 10,000 *akçe*s, he considered middle level; 16 percent, with 10,000–100,000 *akçe*s, rich. İnalcık finally defined a category of the very rich, big merchants, money-changers, jewellers, and silk weavers, 1.3 percent of the cases, who held more than 2,000 ducats or 100,000 *akçe*s.[43] Studying the same city on the basis of the same sources but almost two centuries later, after a severe inflation around 1600, Haim Gerber concluded that a person with an estate of less than 20,000 *akçe*s was poor. Gerber's middle group held 20,000–100,000 *akçe*s and the rich held more than 100,000 *akçe*s.[44] According to these estimates, an estate of 100,000 *akçe*s in the fifteenth century is considered immense and even after the inflation and devaluation of the *akçe* toward the end of the sixteenth century this amount is still in the highest category.

Turning now to the examples of estates left behind by *sancak-beyi* published by Barkan we are in a better position to appreciate the magnitude of the amounts involved. One example is from the year 1606, in a very turbulent period, part of the seventeenth century when a different situation emerged. Of the other two *sancakbeyi*, one was a Sinan Bey who died in 1553 when he was *voynuk sancakbeyi*.[45] This post was perhaps the lowest in the governor rank, and implies that either Sinan Bey died very young or that he spent most of his career in lower ranks before he became *voynuk* commander. Although Barkan thinks the list is not complete, because there was no final accounting and division of property among heirs, Sinan Bey's estate as listed still amounted to about 100,000 *akçe*s.[46] This amount, in view of the official classification of income groups and in terms of İnalcık's findings, places Sinan Bey in İnalcık's very rich category.

In the next example the amount is truly staggering: we find that Yunus Bey, who died in 1572 when he was *sancakbeyi* of Köstendil (in Macedonia), left eight sons, four daughters, and property totalling 1,142,634 *akçe*s.[47] This was the amount to be distributed among the legal heirs after costs had been deducted. In addition, Yunus Bey directly bequeathed some cash, numerous houses in various locations, and set free a number of his slaves. According to the Islamic law of inheritance which applied, he had the right to bequeath one-third of his estate, while two-thirds had to be legally distributed. Assuming that the unspecified values of his various bequests equaled the legally allowed one-third, Yunus Bey's total estate can be computed at 1,713,951 *akçe*s. Quite clearly this amount is in a category of its own, out of all comparison with the subjects, even the wealthiest of the merchants. For this reason İnalcık concluded, in a study on capital accumulation in Ottoman society, that members of the military-administrative group controlled by far the greatest wealth and economic resources.[48]

The contents of the estate lists are instructive as well. In Barkan's categories of analysis, Sinan Bey's relatively small estate comprised household and personal effects (40 percent), six male slaves and one female (18.5 percent), and agricultural materials including stores and implements (41.5 percent). It seems that an analytical category of "professional materials" would have been in order. It would include arms and armor, tents, riding horses, which Barkan cites among household and personal effects, as well as pack animals, at least part of the food and grain stores and the livestock that Barkan considers under the rubric of agricultural investment but which any commander would need and consume in the course of duty on campaigns.[49] According to Barkan's analysis Yunus Bey's estate included household and personal effects worth 231,724 *akçes* (20.3 percent), ten male and two female slaves worth 52,955 *akçes* (4.6 percent), and agricultural investment, 101,086 *akçes* (8.9 percent). The dozens of coats of armor, helmets, spears, the seven tents, the many camel and mule trains, horses furnished for the use of some slaves and household functionaries, the horse trimmings, some of the rolls of cloth (clothing for retainers), some of the livestock and grain stores would be better placed in the proposed category of professional investment. In any case, by far the largest portion of the estate, 756,000 *akçes* (66.2 percent), was kept in cash, mostly in gold pieces; Barkan rightly assumes that this indicates that the *bey* engaged in money-lending.

It should be stressed once again that it is difficult to estimate the average income of a bey, both because his official revenues are for the maintenance of a fairly extensive retinue and because he had unofficial income in the form of booty and from such economic activities as money-lending and grain and livestock speculation. It is clear, however, judging from their estates, that they were as a group the richest men in Ottoman society, that taxes in kind yielded enormous quantities of grain stores, beyond the needs of the household, and that they held farming estates and engaged in agricultural investment. In supplying the needs of the household they also handled large quantities of cloth and other manufactured goods and may have indulged in the trade of such goods as well.

Finally, we should discuss the ways in which such wealth was passed on from generation to generation. The examples published by Barkan show that the legacies of the *ümerā* were subject to Islamic rules of inheritance; in this they were no different than other Muslims, whether members of the ulema (religious-administrative) or simple citizens. A wife—sometimes wives—received one-eighth, daughters half the share of the sons; and other relatives were included among the heirs. There was no differentiation among sons or daughters as to age: children of age and under age received identical shares. The property of a commander would be expropriated by the sultan only if he had been executed for a crime, not a common occurrence in the sixteenth century. If a *bey* died without heirs, his property would be taken over by the sultan; in this the *ümerā* were different from other subjects of the sultan. In the case of a *reāyā* dying without heirs, his property would be taken into the public treasury (*beyt ül-māl*) rather than going directly to the sultan. If we return to a consideration of Yunus Bey's estate, his property was divided among his eight sons and four daughters, some of whom were under age. If any of the sons were already in military-administrative careers, they were not so identified, nor did they receive any of their father's "professional goods," such as the arms, armor, and pack animals.

Sometimes the pious foundation (*vakıf*) system was used to contravene the inheritance laws, by naming specific members of the family or someone else as beneficiaries with substantial allotments. But it was extremely rare among the *ümerā* to put all property in a *vakıf* with family members as the only beneficiaries, a common practice among ordinary citizens.[50] The major portion of the *ümerā vakıfs* went to support charitable institutions that they set up; family members, if at all favored, were usually made administrators of the *vakıf* and sometimes received direct benefits. It was as if it were not worthy of their honor and their high position in society to set up family *vakıfs*, like common people, without establishing charitable works. Noblesse oblige, one might say, being careful to remember that there was no Ottoman nobility. An Ottoman official hoped his name would live on through his charity, not necessarily through his offspring.

Even though *ümerā* sons had an edge over others in the military-administrative career, after the initial advantage, they were on their own and had to prove themselves to get ahead. The inheritance system, too, worked to disburse accumulated wealth among heirs. The result was that, with the exception of some frontier families, there were few examples of members of the same family in prominence for more than two or three generations. From the sixteenth century and into the seventeenth the system experienced what Itzkowitz has called a "hardening of career arteries." Even then, when family and household connections became much more important than before, Ottoman public life remained open to talent and ability. More and more, however, such obscure talent had to be sponsored in a well-established household. Changes in the structure and working of the *ümerā* career, analyzed in the following chapter, favored the rise of households, other than the imperial palace, to even greater prominence.

CHAPTER 4

The Structure of the Military-Administrative Career

WE HAVE SEEN that the *ümerā* had various social origins. But how did the relative importance of these sources change over time? What ranks did the candidates have to hold before attaining those of *sancakbeyi* and *beylerbeyi*? At what level did the palace officials join provincial administration? Registers where all appointments to *ümerā* ranks throughout the empire were recorded provide the data on which to base our answers to such questions. (See appendix 2 for a full discussion of the appointment registers utilized in this study.)

The earliest of these registers (MAD 563) also contains regular entries for certain lesser provincial officers. These include, on one hand, the two *timar* officials in each province, one responsible for keeping the *timar* registers (*timar defterdārı*) and the other the "steward" of the *zeāmet* holders in the provincial capital (*timar kethüdāsı*), and on the other hand the commanders of certain auxiliary troops in Anadolu province (*yaya ve müsellem beyleri*). The career backgrounds of new appointees to these offices are shown in table 4.1. The striking feature of the table is that in the 1560s fully three-quarters of the new appointees to these middle-level provincial positions were from palace administration or from other central government positions, almost totally occupying the posts of *yaya* and *müsellem* commanders. Although still a minority, officers from provincial administration, because their previous experience

TABLE 4.1. Career Backgrounds of New Appointees to Certain Lesser
Provincial Offices in Seven Sample Provinces, 1568–1574

	Timar Kethüdāsı Timar Defterdārı	Yaya *and* Müsellem Commanders	Total (%)
Central Administration	*19*	*19*	*38* (74.5%)
Kapıkulu Officers	2	14	
Müteferrika	5(4a)	—	
Other *Bīrūn* Officers	11	5	
Others	1	—	
Provincial Administration	*12*	*1*	*13* (25.5%)
Zaīm	5(3a)	1	
Others	7	—	
Total	*31*	20	51 (100.0%)
Total[a]	7	—	7 (13.7%)

SOURCE: MAD 563.

[a] *Ümerā* son or relative.

was more valuable here, had a much greater hope of being promoted to the posts of *timar kethüdāsı* and *timar defterdārı*: they made
up 38.7 percent (12 in 31) of appointments to these posts. This is
important for, as we shall see (table 4.2), there were no promotions
to *sancakbeyi* ranks from among the *yaya* and *müsellem* commanders.
These posts, then, must have been dead-end positions for officers
from the palace outside service, especially lesser *kapıkulu* officers.
Here were persons who had survived several selections in their
careers, but who were now deemed not quite capable of holding
higher offices. The *timar defterdārı* and the *timar kethüdāsı*, on the
other hand, could hope to be promoted further; officers reaching
these posts from lesser ranks of provincial administration had a
greater chance of promotion than the totals in table 4.2 at first
indicate. Nevertheless, the fact remains that, in comparison, palace
and central government officials were better placed for promotion
to higher provincial administration ranks, for they still made up
61.3 percent of the appointments to posts of *timar defterdārı* and *timar
kethüdāsı*.

Another point that emerges from the table is that only 13.7
percent of appointments involved sons or other relatives of *ümera*,
and that all seven *ümera* relations, whether from central or provin-

TABLE 4.2. Career Backgrounds of New *Sancakbeyi* in Seven Sample Provinces, 1568–1574

	RE	KA	BU	AN	RM	ER	HL	TOTAL
Central Administration	4	4	2	6	3	—	—	19 (32.2%)
Kapıkulu Officers	1	—	1	3	2	—	—	7
Müteferrika	3(1a)	—	—	—	—	—	—	3
Other Birūn Officers	—	1	1	1	1	—	—	4
Imperial Captains	—	2	—	2	—	—	—	4
Others	—	1	—	—	—	—	—	1
Provincial Administration	1	2	12	8	1	8	8	40 (67.8%)
Alaybeyi	—	—	5	1	—	1	—	7
Zaīm	—	—	2(2a)	—	1(1a)	2(2a)	1(1a)	6
Timar Kethüdāsı	1	—	1	3(1a)	—	2	4	11
Captain	—	2	—	1	—	—	—	3
Hazine Defterdārı	—	—	—	3	—	—	1	4
Others	—	—	4	—	—	3	2	9
TOTAL	5	6	14	14	4	8	8	59 (100.0%)
Total[a]	1	—	2	1	1	2	1	8 (13.6%)

SOURCE: MAD 563.

Note: RE: Rumeli; KA: Kaptan Paşa (Aegean); BU: Budin; AN: Anadolu; RM: Rum (Sivas); ER: Erzurum; HL: Halep (Aleppo).
[a] *Ümerā* son or relative.

TABLE 4.3. Career Backgrounds of New *Sancakbeyi* in Seven Sample Provinces, 1578–1588

	RE	KA	BU	AN	RM	ER	HL	TOTAL
Central Administration	10	5	6	1	2	0	1	25 (44.6%)
Kapıkulu Officers	2	—	1	—	—	—	—	3
Müteferrika	3(3a)	1(1b)	1	1(1a)	1(1a)	—	—	7
Other *Bīrūn* Officers	4(1b)	—	3	—	1	—	1	9
Imperial Captains	1	3(1a)	—	—	—	—	—	4
Others	—	1	1	—	—	—	—	2
Provincial Administration	7	4	5	3	2	3	4	28 (50.0%)
Alaybeyi	—	—	2(1a)	—	—	1	1	2
Zaīm	2(1a)	—	2	1	1	1(1a)	1	5
Timar Kethüdāsı	—	1	—	—	—	—	1	7
Timar Defterdārı	—	3	—	—	1	—	—	2
Captain	1	—	—	—	—	—	—	3
Hazine Defterdārı	3	1	1	2	—	—	—	2
Others	—	—	—	—	—	1	—	7
Ūmerā Related	—	—	—	—	—	1	—	2 (3.6%)
Ūmerā son[a]	—	—	—	—	—	1(1a)	—	1
Household officer[b]	—	1(1b)	—	—	—	—	—	1
Outside the realm	—	—	1	—	—	—	—	1 (1.8%)
TOTAL	17	10	12	4	4	4	5	56 (100.0%)
Total (a) + (b)	6	3	1	1	1	2	—	14 (25%)
(a)	5	1	1	1	1	2	—	11
(b)	1	2	—	—	—	—	—	3

SOURCE: KK 262.

Note: RE: Rumeli; KA: *Kaptan Pāsa* (Aegean); BU: Budin; AN: Anadolu; RM: Rum (Sivas); ER: Erzurum; HL: Halep (Aleppo).

a *Ūmerā* son or relative.
b *Ūmerā* household officer.

TABLE 4.4. Career Backgrounds of New *Sancakbeyi* in Interior and Frontier Regions

	1568–1574			1578–1588			Overall		
	Center	Province	Total	Center	Province	Total	Center	Province	Total
Interior Regions	17	12	29	18	16	35[a]	35	28	64[a]
Percent	*58.6*	*41.4*	*100.0*	*51.4*	*45.7*	*100.0*	*54.7*	*43.8*	*100.0*
RE	4	1	5	10	7	17	14	8	22
KA	4	2	6	5	4	10[a]	9	6	16[a]
AN	6	8	14	1	3	4	7	11	18
RM	3	1	4	2	2	4	5	3	8
Frontier Regions	2	28	30	7	12	21[a]	9	40	51[a]
Percent	*6.7*	*93.3*	*100.0*	*33.3*	*57.1*	*100.0*	*17.6*	*78.4*	*100.0*
BU	2	12	14	6	5	12[a]	8	17	26[a]
ER	—	8	8	—	3	4[a]	—	11	12[a]
HL	—	8	8	1	4	5	1	12	13
Total	19	40	59	25	28	56[a]	44	68	115[a]
Percent	*32.2*	*67.8*	*100.0*	*44.6*	*50.0*	*100.0*	*38.3*	*59.1*	*100.0*

SOURCE: Summary of tables 4.2 and 4.3.

[a] Includes person(s) in other category(ies).

cial administration, were appointed to posts of *timar defterdārı* and *timar kethüdāsı*, open to further promotions. This low percentage is almost exactly the same for *sancakbeyi* appointments (table 4.2), down from more than 40 percent in the 1520s (table 3.3). The obvious conclusion is that being related to other *ümerā* became, in the course of the sixteenth century, much less important for pro- motion in the provincial administration. A different explanation of this sudden dip in the percentage of *ümerā* relations may be that in the 1560s the scribes were more interested in recording the career backgrounds of new appointees and no longer recorded family connections regularly. According to this explanation, there may have been more *ümerā* relations, not identified as such, appointed to provincial ranks. However, even if this were true, by omitting mention of family connections, it leads to the same conclusion: they were no longer significant, at least not significant enough to be recorded. But this relative disregard of family connections in the mid-sixteenth century was only a temporary phenomenon; we shall see that the percentage of new appointees related to other *sancak- beyi*s rose steadily from the 1560s on (tables 4.3 and 4.4).

At the *sancakbeyi* level the relative weight of officers from the central administration and from the provincial administration was the reverse of that in the case of lesser provincial officials. Here more than two-thirds of new appointees were from the lower ranks of provincial administration. This shows that in the 1560s transfers from central to provincial administration took place primarily below the *sancakbeyi* level; in other words, it was expected of most people promoted to the *sancakbeyi* rank, even if they had previously held positions in palace service or in the central government, that they have some experience in provincial government. There was a marked change in this general expectation in the seventeenth century which was already apparent in the 1580s. In barely a decade, from about the 1570s to the 1580s, the ratio of new *sancakbeyi* from provincial administration ranks fell from two-thirds to half of all new appointees, while the share of those from central administration rose to 44.6 percent. However, this rise does not equal the drop in the percentage of the first group; among the groups promoted to *sancakbeyi* in the period 1578–1588 there were two new ones. Although these new groups were very small, they are both important as first instances of new trends that would develop. One was a single, quite exceptional case: an Austrian turncoat who, as reward, was given a *sancak* in Budin province, on the Austrian frontier. The second group, made up of *ümerā*-related persons who were appointed *sancakbeyi* without holding any previous state position, is more interesting in pointing to new developments in the socio-political structure. These persons, together with other *ümerā*-related officers who had held official posts previously, made up a full quarter of all new appointees, thus reversing the trend in the mid-century. There was also a change between these two periods in the manner in which the *ümerā* relations attained the rank of *sancakbeyi*. In the first period only one out of eight such persons had been previously employed in palace service, as a *müteferrika*; all others had first gained experience in provincial administration. In the 1580s, however, of the twelve *ümerā*-related officials who had had previous official (state) experience, two-thirds had served in central government, six as *müteferrika*. The *ümerā* sons, it appears, were no longer required to have experience in provincial administration before they could be appointed *sancakbeyi*.

Especially in the 1570s, officers with a particular kind of official experience were appointed to particular regions (table 4.4). Almost all—twenty-eight out of thirty—*sancakbeyi* appointments in what may be considered frontier provinces, Budin, Erzurum, and Halep (Aleppo), were from the ranks of lesser provincial officials. It seems to have been a requirement of the general character of such areas that the *sancakbeyi* be well-versed in the problems of the region. The other side of the coin was that almost all—seventeen of nineteen—officials from central administration were sent to interior regions. The requirement that border-province *sancakbeyi* be seasoned provincial officials seems to have been relaxed in the second period when central administration officers comprised fully a third of all appointments to *sancaks* in the frontier regions. Nevertheless, three-quarters to the officers promoted to *sancakbeyi* directly from central administration remained in interior regions.

TABLE 4.5. Career Backgrounds of New *Sancakbeyi*, 1570–1640

	1568–1574	1578–1588	1632–1641
Central Administration	*19* (32.2%)	*25* (44.6%)	*31* (49.2%)
Kapıkulu officers	7	3	6
Müteferrika	3(1a)	7(5a, 1b)	11(1a, 1b)
Other *birūn* officers	4	9(1b)	11(3a)
Imperial captains	4	4(1a)	—
Enderūn	—	—	2
Others	1	2	1
Provincial Administration	*40* (67.8%)	*28* (50.0%)	*16* (25.4%)
Alaybeyi	7	2	8
Zāim	6(6a)	5(3a)	5(2a)
Timar kethüdāsı	11(1a)	7(1a)	—
Timar defterdārı	—	2	—
Captain	3	3	—
Hazine defterdārı	4	2	—
Tribal chief	—	—	1
Others	9	7	2
Ümerā Related	—	2 (3.6%)	10 (15.9%)
Ümerā son	—	1	3
Household officers	—	1	7
Outside the Realm	—	1 (1.8%)	6 (9.5%)
TOTAL	*59* (100.0%)	*56* (100.0%)	*63* (100.0%)
(a) *Ümerā* son or relative	8	11	9
(b) *Ümerā* household officer	—	3	8
Total (a) + (b)	*8* (13.6%)	*14* (25.0%)	*17* (26.9%)

SOURCE: KK 266 and Cev. Dah. 6095, with summaries of tables 4.2 and 4.3.

Various trends, first discerned from the 1570s to the 1580s, became much more prominent by the 1630s (table 4.5). The decrease in the share of provincial officers among the new *sancakbeyi*, from 67.8 percent around 1570 to 50.0 percent in the 1580s, quickened at the turn of the century until this share dropped to a mere quarter of all new appointments in the 1630s. In other words, while in the sixteenth century experience in lower provincial offices was highly desirable if not required for promotion to the *sancakbeyi* rank, in the seventeenth century it became almost irrelevant; lower ranks of the provincial administration became in effect a dead-end in terms of *ümerā* careers since almost three-quarters of all new *sancakbeyi* came from other backgrounds. This is a dramatic illustration of the general decline of the *timar* system at the turn of the century, and, as well, of lower-level provincial administration directly related to it.

The increase in the share of the central government officers, too, continued, though at a slower rate. The main increase came between 1570 and 1580, from 32.2 percent to 44.6 percent; until the 1630s the gain was only 5 percent. But the interesting new development from the sixteenth to the seventeenth century was that some pages from the palace inner service (*enderūn*) were sent forth directly to become *sancakbeyi*s, without any intervening experience either in provincial or in central administration. In the *ümerā*-related group as well the main increase came between the first two periods, from 13.6 percent to 25.0 percent, their share in the 1630s being only very slightly higher, 26.9 percent. But here, too, the interesting development is in the manner in which such persons reached the *sancakbeyi* rank. In the 1630s ten out of seventeen were appointed *sancakbeyi* directly from *ümerā* households (15.9 percent of all new appointments); furthermore almost half (eight out of seventeen) were not blood relatives but *ümerā*-household officers, all except one directly promoted to *sancakbeyi* rank without having held any previous state office. This implies that in the seventeenth century service in private households came to be considered a regular alternative to service in the imperial palace— the sultan's household. One other source of *sancakbeyi* which increased its share from the 1580s to the 1630s is made up of those who were not Ottomans at all. These people were high officials of the neighboring rival empires, Safavi in the 1630s, who joined the Ottoman empire and were rewarded by the grant of *sancaks*. They, and the single case in the 1580s of the turncoat Austrian, reflect the special wartime conditions in the 1580s and the 1630s on both the Austrian and Iranian fronts.

In promotions to *beylerbeyi* rank, too, the trends discerned from the sixteenth to the seventeenth century are parallel to changes we have noted in *sancakbeyi* appointments. The numbers of new *beylerbeyi* on which to base our observations are admittedly small; nevertheless it will be seen that the directions of change are unmistakably clear. It is striking, for example, that around 1570 85.7

TABLE 4.6. Career Backgrounds of New Beylerbeyi, 1570–1640

	1568–1574	*1578–1588*	*1632–1641*
Central Administration	*3* (14.3%)	*7* (35.0%)	*32* (61.5%)
Kapıkulu officers	2	2	9
Other *Bīrūn* officers	—	3	13
Enderūn pages	—	—	9
Others	1	2	1
Provincial Administration	*18* (85.7%)	*11* (55%)	*14* (26.9%)
Sancakbeyi	18(4a)	8(2a, 1b)	14(1a, 4b)
Others	—	3	—
Ümerā Household Officers	—	—	3 (5.8%)
Outside the Realm	—	2 (10%)	3 (5.8%)
TOTAL	*21* (100.0%)	*20* (100.0%)	*52* (100.0%)
(a) *Ümerā* son or relative	4	2	1
(b) *Ümerā* household officers	—	1	7
Total (a) + (b)	*4* (19.0%)	*3* (15.0%)	*8* (15.4%)

SOURCE: *Ümerā* appointment registers.

percent of all new *beylerbeyi* are from among the *sancakbeyi*: with very few exceptions it seems to have been the rule in that period for officers to serve first in provincial administration before being considered worthy of promotion to the *beylerbeyi* rank. This requirement, which incidentally points out the importance and prestige the *sancakbeyi* enjoyed in the mid-sixteenth century, was relaxed by the 1580s. By then the share of *sancakbeyi* among new *beylerbeyi* was down to 55 percent, while the share of central administrative officers jumped from 14.3 percent to 35.0 percent. The two persons in the new "outside the realm" category were again officers of rival empires enticed to join the Ottoman state during the eastern campaigns in the 1580s.

These trends continued at the same rate from the 1580s to the 1630s: the share of the *sancakbeyi* plummeted to 26.9 percent while that of the central administration personnel climbed to 61.5 percent. Furthermore, within this group were now some pages from the palace inner (*enderūn*) service, not an insignificant group at 17.3 percent of total new appointments, promoted directly to *beylerbeyi* rank. A second major trend was that, although the percentage of persons related to *ümerā* remained stable, more officers from *ümerā* households, rather than *ümerā* sons, were appointed, some without any service in state offices.

The changes in the *ümerā* career lines that we have been noting are reflected in chart 4.1 which should be compared with chart 3.1. The striking thing about chart 4.1 must be its confusion: this confusion indicates that the measured flexibility of the system in the mid-sixteenth century had turned into a nonsystem with no regular lines because almost anybody could move to almost any part of the structure. But within this general confusion some important new elements should be underlined. One major new development was the rise of the *ümerā* households as an important source of manpower for *ümerā* ranks. This was not so much due to an increase in numbers, though certainly that was true; but to the fact that officers from *ümerā* households could join administration even at the highest levels. A second change was in the way central administration officers were sent out to the provinces. In the sixteenth century they used to join provincial administration at the ranks below *sancakbeyi*; there were few exceptional officers who came out of central administration at *ümerā* ranks. In the seventeenth century, on the other hand, central administration officers, including persons from the *enderūn*, joined provincial administration at the *sancakbeyi* and even *beylerbeyi* rank. As the central administration officers came to take over the *ümerā* ranks, it became increasingly difficult for lesser provincial officers to be promoted: only a quarter of the *sancakbeyi* were from their ranks and only a quarter of the *beylerbeyi* were chosen from among the *sancakbeyi* in the seventeenth century. What these shifts mean in terms of the general transformation of the empire we will be in a better position to understand after we review other aspects of the *ümerā* career.

Duration and Location of *Ümerā* Appointments

Along with the study of changes in manpower sources and manner of promotion, the analysis of conditions of service provides insights into the nature of the change in the *ümerā* career. Table 4.7, for example, shows that the *sancakbeyi* tended to be shifted from one

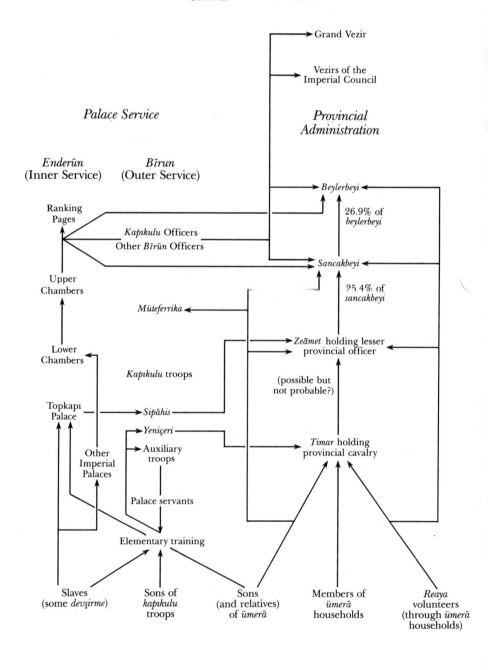

TABLE 4.7. Regionalism in *Sancakbeyi* Appointments

Area	1568–1574				1578–1588				1632–1641			
	RE	AN	TOTAL	%	RE	AN	TOTAL	%	RE	AN	TOTAL	%
From same *sancak*	—	—	—	—	9	17	26	10.2	18	41	59	16.0
From within the same province	49	54	103	41.5	76	21	97	37.9	45	52	97	26.5
From *sancak* of neighboring province	38	53	91	36.7	42	32	74	28.9	26	83	109	29.8
From within region	2	26	28	11.3	19	23	42	16.4	8	68	76	20.8
From outside region	10	16	26	10.5	8	9	17	6.6	10	15	25	6.9
TOTAL	99	149	248	100.0	154	102	256	100.0	107	259	366	100.0

SOURCE: *Ümerā* appointment registers.

Notes: RE: Rumeli general region; AN: Anadolu general region. The Aegean province was considered within both general regions and neighboring both the Rumeli and the Anadolu provinces.

TABLE 4.8. Intervals out of Office between *Sancakbeyi* Appointments

	1568–1574	*1578–1588*	*1632–1641*
One Year	96	41 (87.2%)	82
1 month	87	32 (68.1%)	36
1–4 months	3	3	20
5–8 months	2	3	14
9–12 months	4	3	12
Two Years	3	6 (12.8%)	13
13–16 months	3	1	6
17–20 months	—	3	3
21–24 months	—	2	4
Longer	1	—	5
TOTAL	100	47 (100.0%)	100

SOURCE: Ümerā appointment registers.
Note: All ascertainable intervals for the first two periods (it is a coincidence that intervals ascertained in the period 1568–1574 number exactly 100); first 100 intervals in alphabetical order from 1632 to 1641.

sancak to another either in the same province or in a neighboring province. This was basically true in all three periods under study; more than 70 percent of all *sancakbeyi* appointments were consistently effected in this way. From the 1570s to the 1630s more and more *sancakbeyi* returned to the same *sancak* they had held earlier as there came to be an increasingly longer wait between appointments (table 4.8). It was quite rare, though less so later on, for a *sancakbeyi* to be appointed to another province even in the same region. As for inter-regional transfers, they became even more exceptional by the seventeenth century.

While the regionalism of the *sancakbeyi* appointments remained stable from the sixteenth to the seventeenth centuries, the duration of office was increasingly shorter (table 4.9). This development was a subject of complaint in the seventeenth century; indeed, some Ottoman political commentators cited shorter terms of office as a basic ill of the system.[1] The ratio of *sancakbeyi* dismissed from one post within one or two years rose from 28 and 57 percent respectively in the first period to 44 and 82 percent in the second and reached 55 and 89 percent in the 1630s. It should be noted that the significant change in the percentages comes between the 1570s and the 1580s; the rate of increase is slower between the

TABLE 4.9. Duration of Office for *Sancakbeyi*

	1568–1574	*1578–1588*	*1632–1641*
One Year	*28*	*44*	*55*
4 months	8	15	15
5–8 months	7	15	19
9–12 months	13	14	21
Two Years	*29*	*38*	*34*
13–16 months	15	15	15
17–20 months	3	13	11
21–24 months	11	10	8
Three Years	*21*	*12*	*7*
25–30 months	11	8	4
31–36 months	10	4	3
Longer	22	*6*	*4*
TOTAL	100	100	100

SOURCE: Ümerā appointment registers.
Note: First 100 appointments in alphabetical order.

last two periods. The major drop in the percentage of terms of office longer than three years, too, was between the first two periods. While around 1570 there were quite a few *sancakbeyi* (22 percent) who served at one post more than three years, both in the 1580s and in the 1630s such long terms of office were quite exceptional (6 and 4 percent respectively) and occurred only in *sancaks* which were themselves exceptional because they were in frontier regions or because they had a special status. Incidentally, the fact that in all three periods length of office was not so much in annual intervals but rather that the *sancakbeyi* could be dismissed at any time of year indicates that appointments were not effected in any particular season.

It can be observed in table 4.8 that while the length of office grew shorter, the *sancakbeyi* spent longer periods out of office between appointments. The percentage of *sancakbeyi* who were reappointed, after being dismissed from one particular post, within a month, usually immediately, went down from 87 percent around the 1570s to 68.1 percent in the 1580s and as low as 36 percent in the 1630s. The decrease in the percentage of those reappointed within a year was not nearly so drastic; even in the 1630s 82 percent of the *sancakbeyi* were given another post within a year. The fact remains, however, that a majority were out of office for several months. It should be added that intervals can be determined so long as the various offices a particular *sancakbeyi* held in succession can be identified. In the registers KK262 and especially in KK266 and Cev. Dah. 6095, which supply the data for the two later periods, there are many omissions, making it sometimes impossible to identify all the offices one *sancakbeyi* held unless they were in immediate succession. More longer intervals went unidentified and thus the change from around 1570 on was even greater than table 4.8 indicates.

Staying for a shorter term at a given post and having to spend months, even years, before another appointment, obviously hurt the *sancakbeyi* financially. Later we shall have to relate this development to other changes in the economic position of the *ümerā*. However, reviewing the trends in the location and duration of *sancakbeyi* appointments we can observe certain features of the *ümera* career. For one thing, it seems quite definite that a basic principle of *sancakbeyi* appointments was not to allow an officer to remain at one post for any length of time: even around 1570, 78 percent of the *sancakbeyi* were dismissed within three years. We can surmise that this was done to prevent an officer from establishing himself too securely in any one region by forming close ties with regional political and economic power-holders. On the other hand, the tendency to move a *sancakbeyi* within the same province or to a neighboring province probably reflects the considerations that a *sancakbeyi* should not spend too much time during his transfer so as not to leave a *sancak* untended for too long and, more importantly, that the *sancakbeyi* should gain experience within a general region and should be familiar with its particular problems. Even if this last point was not an articulated consideration, the consequence of transferring a *sancakbeyi* within the same region throughout his career was precisely that he became an expert, so to speak, on that region.

In the appointment of the *beylerbeyi*, too, there was a degree of regionalism; around 90 percent of *beylerbeyi* appointments were within one of the two general regions fairly consistently throughout the three periods (table 4.10). One change throughout the periods

TABLE 4.10. Regionalism in *Beylerbeyi* Appointments

	1568–1574				1578–1588				1632–1641			
	RE	AN	TOTAL	%	RE	AN	TOTAL	%	RE	AN	TOTAL	%
From same province	—	—	—	—	—	—	—	—	5	6	11	10.0
From *Sancak* of same province	—	—	—	—	—	1	1	1.8	1	8	9	8.2
From neighboring province	—	15	15	30.6	3	15	18	32.2	8	14	22	20.0
From *Sancak* of neighboring province	1	4	5	10.2	—	2	2	3.6	2	8	10	9.1
From province within region	—	16	16	32.7	2	23	25	44.6	4	24	28	25.5
From *Sancak* within region	1	7	8	16.3	2	3	5	8.9	3	12	15	13.6
From province outside region	—	1	1	2.0	3	1	4	7.1	6	6	12	10.9
From *Sancak* outside region	—	4	4	8.2	—	1	1	1.8	2	1	3	2.7
TOTAL	2	47	49	100.0	10	46	56	100.0	31	79	110	100.0

SOURCE: Ümerā appointment registers.

Note: RE: Rumeli general region; AN: Anadolu general region.

TABLE 4.11. Intervals Out of Office between Beylerbeyi Appointments

	1568–1574				1578–1588				1632–1641			
	Out of Office	With Arpalık	Total	%	Out of Office	With Arpalık	Total	%	Out of Office	With Arpalık	Total	%
One Year	21	2	23	95.8	10	—	10	90.9	23	15	38	70.4
to 1 month	21	—	21	87.5	9	—	9	81.8	13	—	13	24.1
2–4 months	—	1	1	4.2	—	—	—		3	5	8	14.8
5–8 months	—	—	—		—	—	—		2	4	6	11.1
9–12 months	—	1	1	4.2	1	—	1	9.1	5	6	11	20.4
Two Years	—	—	—		1	—	1	9.1	1	10	11	20.4
12–16 months	—	—	—		1	—	1	9.1	—	4	4	7.4
17–20 months	—	—	—		—	—	—		—	2	2	3.7
21–24 months	—	—	—		—	—	—		1	4	5	9.3
Longer	—	1	1	4.2	—	—	—		1	4	5	9.3
TOTAL	21	3	24	100.0	11	—	11	100.0	25	29	54	100.0

SOURCE: Ümerā appointment registers.

is the increase in the number of *beylerbeyi* returning to the post he had vacated some time earlier, which of course is related to the increase in the percentage of those *beylerbeyi* who had to spend some time out of office between appointments (table 4.11). This development has already been noted for the *sancakbeyi*, but unlike the *sancakbeyi* this phenomenon had developed for the *beylerbeyi* only by the 1630s. Similarly, the decrease in the length of time spent at a particular post is more dramatic in the case of the *beylerbeyi* between the 1580s and the 1630s. While it is true that the percentage of *beylerbeyi* who served at one post more than two years decreased drastically between the 1570s and the 1580s, the majority (53.3 percent) still served between one and two years in the 1580s whereas close to 60 percent were dismissed within a year in the 1630s (table 4.12). The data on the growing intervals between appointments (table 4.11) is much more unequivocal on this point. Both in the 1570s and the 1580s it was a rare *beylerbeyi* who was not appointed to another post immediately, i.e., within a month, after dismissal; in the third period less than a quarter were so appointed and almost a third of the *beylerbeyi* had to wait more than one year before reappointment to a province. To alleviate the financial burden on the *beylerbeyi* who had to spend any length of time out of

TABLE 4.12. Duration of Office For *Beylerbeyi*

	1568–1574	*1578–1588*	*1632–1641*
One Year	*9* (23.1%)	*5* (33.3%)	*60* (59.4%)
4 months	1	1	20
5–8 months	4	—	18
9–12 months	4	4	22
Two Years	*11* (28.2%)	*8* (53.3%)	*31* (30.6%)
13–16 months	3	3	10
17–20 months	2	2	11
21–24 months	6	3	10
Three Years	*7* (17.9%)	*1* (6.7%)	*7* (7%)
25–30 months	4	1	4
31–36 months	3	—	3
Longer	*12* (30%)	*1* (6.7%)	*3* (3%)
TOTAL	*39* (*100.0%*)	*15* (*100.0%*)	*101* (*100.0%*)

SOURCE: Ümerā appointment registers.

office the state at least allowed them some official revenues by assigning them *sancak*s as "*arpalık*," literally "fodder money." In the 1630s, of the forty-one *beylerbeyi* who were not immediately reappointed twenty-nine (70.7 percent) were assigned *sancak*s in this manner; this ratio went up to fourteen out of sixteen (87.5 percent) for those out of office longer than a year.

The simultaneous decrease in the length of tenure at one post and increase of the interval between appointments from the sixteenth century to the seventeenth is a distinct indication of a congestion in the *ümerā* career. On the basis of the data supplied by the *ümerā* appointment registers we can determine that this congestion first obtained at the *sancakbeyi* level, quite suddenly, between the 1570s and the 1580s; by the 1630s at the *beylerbeyi* level, too, there was a serious problem of overcrowding. The slowing down of conquests from about the middle of the sixteenth century can be cited as a cause of this congestion, as has been done, but it is only part of the explanation. We have also discovered, in our analysis of *ümerā* career lines, that in the second half of the sixteenth century manpower sources for the military-administrative elite became more varied. From the 1550s on not only were few new posts being created as a result of conquests, but there were more candidates for *ümerā* positions. Furthermore, persons from new sources such as *ümerā* households came to join the military-administrative structure at ever higher ranks, competing with candidates awaiting promotion from lower levels of provincial administration. At first the proliferation of manpower sources may have been due to the assumption of continuing growth, an assumption further encouraged by the vast acquisitions in the early decades of the sixteenth century. But even after realities disproved this assumption at the turn of the century, persons from new channels kept flooding the system. Clearly, these channels, once opened, could not now be checked; there were new forces at work which required them to be kept open. One source of manpower which could readily be closed was the *devşirme*. Predictably, the *devşirme* method of recruitment was altogether abandoned in the first half of the seventeenth century.

CHAPTER 5

Transformation of Provincial Administration

THE CONGESTION IN the military-administrative career diagnosed in the preceding chapter placed a financial burden on the *ümerā*. Because tenure at one post was shorter, the expenses involved in moving households and retinues from one post to another were more often incurred. More seriously, the *ümerā* were left without official revenues during the increasingly longer periods spent out of office between appointments. Furthermore, as we shall see in greater detail, even when out of office the *ümerā* were forced to keep large retinues, because at a time when there was greater competition among an increasingly greater number of candidates for not many more, maybe even fewer, offices, the officers who attended campaigns with large households had a better chance of earlier appointment or promotion. The paradox was that the candidate who could afford a large retinue while out of office could get a position and therefore have official revenues with which to increase his household.

These developments in the *ümerā* career took place at a time when the empire came to face a greater military challenge along the western frontiers, both on land and at sea. From the west, along the Mediterranean, came also several waves of inflation, flooding Ottoman markets with silver from the Spanish Empire in the Americas. In the face of the western military challenge and the inflation, many aspects of the Ottoman system needed to be re-organized. Several strands, political, social, and economic, inter-acted to cause the transformation in the *ümerā* career as well as in other institutions of the empire. We will first have to unravel these various strands to see their individual impact, though of course the altered situation in the seventeenth century is the consequence of the cumulative force of several simultaneous, and originally un-related, developments.

In the previous sections we have discerned changes in the *ümerā* career, other things being equal, which of course they were not. One of the most important new elements with considerable impact on the Ottoman state in the sixteenth century was the nature of the enemy faced in the west. During earlier centuries of expansion in the Balkans the Ottomans had conquered relatively weak states with internal discord among religious groups, between serfs and their masters, or between feudal nobles and rulers. After the Ottomans defeated the Hungarian army at Mohacz in 1526 and conquered the land in stages in the following decades, they confronted the Hapsburg Empire and a very different Europe. The religious, social, political, economic, scientific, and technological changes associated with the renaissance and the reformation con-tributed to the development of stronger states, better organized, more unified under the ruler and his central government, and quick to apply scientific advances to military technology. The result was that from about the middle of the sixteenth century Ottoman advance in central Europe came to a standstill.[1] The previously shifting and expanding Ottoman frontier area became a relatively stable border line: on the Hapsburg border there were only minor revisions from the mid-century, with a few frontier outposts changing hands every now and then. Later Ottoman conquests in the west came at the expense of the Venetians: Cyprus was invaded in 1571 and Crete, after a twenty-five year struggle, was finally annexed in 1669.

The Ottomans realized that the Hapsburgs were a formidable enemy. Among various Ottoman treatises on what was wrong with the system, which flourished during the "time of troubles" from the late sixteenth century on, one by a retired *kadı*, written in the

1590s, is especially interesting in this context.[2] The author, Hasan el-Kāfi el-Akhisāri, had spent time in Bosnia, and his knowledge of frontier conditions is evident in his comments.[3] Although the author casts his argument in an Islamic setting—with the fairly standard opening of the relation of a dream in which the prophet Muhammad appeared to him—and deplores what he perceives to be a growing disregard of Islamic principles of law, he also comments on the military conditions of the frontier. The Austrians, he says, are better organized than they used to be, better disciplined, and as cunning as the devil, always inventing ingenious weapons and siege engines. He observes that the Ottomans, on the other hand, used to adopt such new weapons quite readily in the old days, but now, let alone making and using new weapons and techniques, they do not even train sufficiently in the use of their traditional weapons.

A European observer, Busbecq, who lived in the Ottoman realm in the 1550s as the ambassador of the Hapsburg emperor Charles V, relates that the grand vezir of the time had recently attempted to create a new corps of musket-bearing cavalry as a response to the Hapsburg challenge in central Europe.[4] The attempt failed because the cavalrymen selected for the project were ridiculed by their peers and simply refused to carry the muskets. The infantry, *yeniçeri*s, had employed firearms routinely since early in the fifteenth century; indeed Ottoman use of firearms and field artillery was a major element in their success, early in the sixteenth century, over such formidable Islamic rivals as the Mamluks of Egypt and the Safavis of Iran.[5] The refusal of the imperial cavalry (*sipāhi*s) to carry muskets may have been due to their higher status in the Ottoman army than the *yeniçeri*s, and to the messy and unchivalrous nature of the muskets. In any case, Busbecq's account indicates the Ottomans felt the need for new techniques as early as the mid-century.

The second half of the sixteenth century witnessed a considerable growth in the size of the central army, as part of the Ottoman response to the Hapsburg challenge. The various corps of the sultan's household troops, which had numbered about 15,000 a century earlier, grew to 40,000 by around 1570 and to 85,000 by the end of the century.[6] Simultaneously, the importance of the provincial cavalry declined, for *timar* holders, dispersed over the countryside, could not be brought together for drills and training in new weapons and tactics. The rise of the central army in numbers and the decline of the provincial cavalry in effectiveness had important financial consequences. The central army troops were paid in cash; the state also paid for their expenses both in war and in peace. As their numbers grew so did the burden on the treasury. A major portion of the state's revenues, however, had been assigned to the provincial cavalry through the *dirlik* system. What was needed, then, from around 1550 to 1650, was a massive operation of transfer of revenues tied up in the *dirlik* system to a tax-farming system of revenue collection. This shift away from assigning revenues in return for services and toward an arrangement which yielded cash to the central treasury was gradual, for it meant nothing less than a total revision of the classic Ottoman system of organizing revenue collection in conjunction with provincial administration and military service.[7] There was no wholesale abolishment of *timars*; they existed well into the nineteenth century. As *timars* fell vacant, however, they were taken over by the central treasury and either consolidated to form tax farms or granted in support of palace and central government personnel. A second major development that accelerated in the course of the century was that cash taxes, *avārız*, collected by the central government only in times of extraordinary need, came to be regularized, standardized, and collected annually. This newly standardized tax was not in lieu of existing ones but in addition to them; in other words the subjects of the empire were to assume the burden of the increased spending of the central treasury.

It has been ascertained that sixteenth-century Ottoman lands also experienced a rapid population growth.[8] Accompanied as it was by a certain increase in agricultural productivity, this growth would not necessarily have led to population pressure; but as the state and, as we shall see, its representatives increased the tax burden on the *reāyā*, the lot of the growing peasant population became quite unbearable.[9] The excess population, pushed off the land, flocked to the cities or crowded rural *medreses*, schools, where they were supported by the college's endowments. These phenomena, common in many developing countries of the contemporary world, contributed to unrest both in the cities and in the countryside. In the 1570s a wave of rural student disturbances started when bands of students descended on villages as uninvited guests. Soon the proportion of such incidents rose to such levels as to be termed uprisings by modern historians.[10] Toward the end of the century rural disturbances took a more serious turn when many young peasants acquired horses and muskets and formed large bands of bandits. The state was willing to hire some of these village youth turned fighters as mercenaries, especially since it had been trying to develop its own musket-bearing cavalry.[11] But such mercenaries were hired seasonally. When they were left without pay after campaigns, many of them contributed to rural unrest.

A development parallel in time was the Mediterranean inflation which reached Ottoman lands in the second half of the sixteenth century. The stages of its impact can be followed in price indexes fashioned by the late Ömer Lütfi Barkan, the foremost Ottoman economic historian.[12] Barkan worked out changes in food prices in Istanbul between 1490 and 1655, first measured in *akçes*, the basic silver coin of the empire, and second in grams silver. The second step was necessitated because, while the inflation raged in the second half of the sixteenth century, the government reduced, on several occasions, the silver content of the *akçe*. Even if there had been no real inflation, therefore, prices in *akçes* would have increased because the value of the coin itself was reduced. The real indicator of the change in the value of goods is the index in grams silver. Nevertheless, the index based on prices in *akçes*, even if not an accurate measure of inflation, is not devoid of significance, for well into the seventeenth century when it was replaced by the *kuruş*, a much bigger silver coin, the *akçe* remained the standard unit of money in which all financial quantities, whether taxes or salaries or prices, were measured. Admittedly these indexes are imperfect guides to the course of the inflation within the empire as they are based only on food prices and only in Istanbul. Even with such serious limitations, however, Barkan's indexes serve as rough yardsticks.

On the basis of Barkan's calculations the course of the inflation can be viewed in three separate waves. The first wave washed Ottoman shores in the period 1556–1573, but it was the second wave, 1588–1597, that truly inundated the lands of the empire. Although the inflation subsided immediately after this, a third and equally violent wave struck in 1615–1625. From then on there were some relatively small increases. Nevertheless, especially after the 1630s, the inflation was by and large brought under control. To illustrate this point, it is interesting to note that values in 1655 were not too different from those in 1588. Even when measured in *akçes* the index of 462 in 1655 (1490 = 100) is not much greater than the 366 points in 1588. In short, it would be safe to say that the highest levels of the indexes reached between 1595 and 1623 were only temporary.[13]

The *Ümerā* in Transition

Inflation, as everybody knows, hits hardest those with fixed incomes, but producers, especially of foodstuffs, may in fact benefit from it. In the Ottoman context this was not necessarily so. Barkan demonstrated that food prices went up and we know from Bruce McGowan's ground-breaking research that Ottoman peasants retained, after paying taxes, a portion of their produce beyond their own needs which they were able to market.[14] The lot of the peasantry, therefore, should not have deteriorated at all. The important question, however, is who controlled the marketable agricultural surplus and who benefited from the rising prices. This question has not yet been posed in Ottoman historiography, much less answered; nevertheless it seems clear that the peasants were not allowed to keep enough beyond subsistence to enjoy the benefit of price increases.

As for "fixed" incomes, after a while they seem to have become fairly meaningless. Central army troops, for example, were paid daily wages the levels of which do not seem to have increased appreciably from the sixteenth to the seventeenth century. As their numbers increased immensely in this period and their payments were already an enormous burden on the treasury, the state was in no position to increase their daily wages. Indeed, their wages continued to be calculated in *akçe*s and there were several serious riots when the state attempted to pay them in the newly devalued coins. The solution was to allow central army troops to augment their salaries through various extracurricular activities: *yeniçeri*s, for example, entered the trades in Istanbul, often using their political muscle in unfair competition with the guilds in the city.[15] The senior troops, the cavalrymen (*sipāhi*s), took on more lucrative positions: they became more involved in tax collection, retaining a share of the revenues; many were appointed as managers (*mütevelli*) or in other capacities to the extensive imperial pious foundations (*vakıf*). Also, especially following the struggles for the throne among Süleyman's sons and during the disturbances towards the end of the century, many central army troops were stationed in the provinces where, because of their political power, they came to be numbered among the provincial notables with extensive economic dealings. Thus, not only on the battlefield but also in the provinces, the central army came to play a greater role, often at the expense of the classical structure of provincial administration.

The provincial administrators, too, had "fixed" incomes in the sense that there seems to have been no increase in the levels of *dirlik*s granted to them. In seventeenth-century lists of *hās* allowed to governors the figures are identical to those of the previous century (see appendix 1). But, as was the case of the central army troops, the fact that the nominal value of a *dirlik* remained unchanged did not mean that real incomes did not increase. Let us look into this a bit more closely. It can be easily noted that while sixteenth-century appointment registers took great care in recording the *hās* a governor held at each post, in later registers the *hās* figures are frequently omitted. This was not because of a relaxation of bureaucratic standards or because the seventeenth-century bureaucrats were more careless than their earlier colleagues— after all, different sorts of information, missing from earlier registers, did come to be included later because these facts were now deemed important and the *hās* a governor held came to be considered almost irrelevant among the earnings of the *ümerā*. It should be emphasized in this context that a portion of the *dirlik* holder's revenues was collected from the subjects as a share of produce, in kind. The *dirlik* holder then marketed the part of this produce that remained after the needs of his household had been met. Thus, while food prices were rising, his income was greater than the nominal value of the *dirlik*.

Since *hās* figures were no longer regularly entered in seventeenth-century registers and since the nominal *hās* was far from being a good indicator of a governor's real revenues, we do not have detailed information on the *ümerā*'s earnings after 1600. There are indications, however, that there was a relative impoverishment, especially among the district governors (*sancakbeyi*), and this was deplored in some sources mainly because the *beys* could not then maintain sufficient retinues. A seventeenth-century historian, Peçuylu İbrahim Efendi, a native of Hungary, had first-hand knowledge of frontier conditions. He notes that booty from raids into enemy territory used to provide huge incomes to *beys* along the frontier and they used to be able to maintain grand households with large retinues. In our day, he writes (in the 1640s), nobody can afford such large households.[16]

Peçuylu was writing about the frontier *ümerā*. It may be thought that this particular group was deprived of special booty income because the Austrians were more powerful and that therefore Peçuylu's comment did not reflect general conditions. We have other testimony, however, that the relative impoverishment of the *ümerā* was a widespread phenomenon. Yemişçi Hasan Paşa, grand vezir from 1601 to 1603, had this to say on the subject in a report to the sultan:

> Your servants the governors do not have power or riches. None of them, whether vezir or *beylerbeyi* or *sancakbeyi*, is able anymore to maintain a proper and large retinue as before. This is why the enemy is victorious. If one of your servants is asked to perform a duty he pleads poverty and asks for huge sums from my glorious sultan. When such of your servants are rich and powerful this is no waste: the benefit of that richness is bound to return to the state and religion.[17]

In other words, what is good for the *ümerā* is good for the state. This was not Hasan Paşa's personal view but a basic element in

Ottoman political thinking: we have seen that the official income
assigned to the *ümerā* was intended to support their retinues as well.

The state, then, had to take steps to ensure that the *ümerā*
could maintain households. One way was to assign state revenues
directly to members of *ümerā* households. This had been done in
earlier times as well; examples from the first half of the sixteenth
century were noted in chapter 3. But towards the end of the
century the practice became widespread. Peçuylu notes resent-
ment among the troops on both the Austrian and the Iranian fronts
when commanders assigned large numbers of *timar*s to their own
men.[18] Ferhad Paşa, commander of the western front, defended his
actions against the reaction of the local troops by noting that his
men deserved *timar*s because they had already served on the eastern
front. He promised, however, that in the future he would assign
only one-third of vacant *timar*s to members of his household!

In addition to *dirlik* grants, it can be observed that members of
ümerā households were also given palace and government positions
at the center, while they were still considered as belonging to a
particular household.[19] Obviously, this development had political
implications far beyond helping out the *ümerā* with their household
expenses: patronage was in time to become of paramount importance in shaping the careers of such household members turned
government official, and the political and personal clashes among
the most prominent Ottomans were to spread to the whole
political-administrative structure.

The fact that many *timar* holders were members of a *paşa*'s
household went against the logic of the *dirlik* system for such *timar*
holders spent most of their time in the *paşa*'s service rather than at
their *timar*s. But a development of a different nature went far more
to undermine the classical system of provincial administration: this
was the granting of certain state revenues to officials on a permanent basis, regardless of where they happened to be serving at a
given time. Such state revenues held continuously were termed
"estate-like" (*ber vech-i çiftlik, bi-resm-i çiftlik*), implying a degree of
proprietary rights which, however, fell short of ownership. I will
dwell on this at some length for the phenomenon has important
implications.

The practice was not entirely new; examples have come from

early in the sixteenth century. The first instance I have come across is in fact dated 894/1488. An entry in the Anatolian *dirlik*-grant register states that an Uçarı Bey was granted a village as an estate (*çiftlik tarikiyle*), as a reward for his services in a recent campaign against the Mamluks.[20] It is not clear what Uçarı Bey's rank was nor whether he held any other state grants. In the sixteenth century the examples concern the *ümerā*: in 929/1522 the *beylerbeyi* of Karaman was allotted 698,884 *akçe*s as *hās* within his province; an additional portion of 14,052 *akçe*s was supplied by seven villages near Edirne in Rumeli province, which were termed the governor's *çiftlik*.[21] Around the middle of the century the practice seems to have become more widespread: in the Rumeli *dirlik*-grant register for the years 948–49/1541–42 there are four instances where the district governor held a portion of his *hās* permanently.[22] In three other examples in the same register the portion held permanently is termed "estate-like" or "as an estate."[23] In one of these cases it is specified that the portion of official revenues held permanently as an estate used to be a *timar*.[24]

In the *ümerā* appointment registers, too, we note the same phenomenon, by then much more prevalent. Indeed, in one example in MAD 563 (pp. 48–49) we can trace the career of a Mehmed Bey while his permanent holdings grew. When he was governor of Pojega he held additional revenues in Semendire and later, when he was transferred to Istolni Belgrad, it was entered that he held permanent revenues in Sirem as well. Unfortunately, just as the practice was spreading the appointment registers started omitting details of *hās* figures and, indeed, any information on the *hās*, so that it becomes impossible to gauge the true extent of *hās* portions held as estates, other than to note that the practice seems to have become much more common by the end of the century.[25]

Such permanent revenues did not amount to a large portion of a *hās*, at most 10 percent of the total, and usually less.[26] But the importance of this practice goes far beyond the figures involved. For one thing, it went against the rationale of the *dirlik* system, which was to achieve as high a degree of correspondence as possible between a *sancakbeyi*'s office and his *hās*. Ideally, all portions of a *hās* should have been in the *sancak* where the *bey* was posted. By allowing him to keep some revenues in a certain *sancak* permanently while he himself moved to a different *sancak*, the portion of revenues in a given district outside the control of the governor was increased. At the same time there were more *ümerā* receiving revenues from districts in which they were not serving.

The exact nature of "estate-like" holdings is not clear.[27] The holder was not an owner. The sultan sometimes did grant state lands in private ownership, but this was done through the process of *temlīk*, granting as property, by means of a document called *temlīknāme*, deed of assignment in private ownership. Such lands were held *ber vech-i mülkiyet*, as private property. Property held *ber vech-i mülkiyet* passed on to heirs or was given in support of a pious foundation (*vakıf*). How was *ber vech-i çiftlik* different from *ber vech-i mülkiyet*? The question is difficult to answer because, just as the phenomenon becomes prevalent in the late sixteenth century, the land and census registers (*tahrīrs*) came to be gradually abandoned so that tracing such holdings through registers may be impossible. Even if "estate-like" holdings were not passed on to heirs, it seems reasonable to assume that they were held at least during an officer's lifetime, otherwise these holdings would be no different than other portions of the *hās*. It is significant that the practice became widespread at a time when *ümerā* came to experience longer periods out of office while waiting for a new appointment: if a *bey* lost the rest of his *hās* he at least had one portion, however small, as an "unemployment benefit" so to speak.

This practice is similar to that of assigning *sancak*s to *beylerbeyi*s as *arpalık*, literally fodder money, to keep them in funds while they waited for a province appointment befitting their rank. In the 1630s certain Anatolian *sancak*s, most prominently Kastamonu, Saruhan, Çorum, Kangırı, and Beyşehri, as well as Jerusalem, were almost invariably assigned as *arpalık*s; they had, in effect, ceased to become regular *sancak*s.[28]

Allowing *ümerā* household members to hold larger numbers of *timar*s, granting *hās* portions as permanent holdings to *ümerā*, and giving *sancak*s as *arpalık* to governors general were all developments, more or less simultaneous, equally against the nature of the classical system of provincial administration. With the decline of

the military status of the provincial cavalry, the central government was not interested in keeping up the *dirlik* system with all its
ramifications. What the center wanted from the provinces was
more cash contributions. The center also expected the *ümerā* to
maintain households and so devised ways to help them. But by and
large the state was not interested in the plight of the *timar* holders
who found it increasingly difficult, at a time of rising costs, to take
part in campaigns paying their own way. There were half-hearted
attempts to provide loans to especially hard-pressed *timar* holders
so they could come to the campaigns and to eliminate the smallest
*timar*s which were no longer viable.[29] But by the middle of the
seventeenth century the state did not seem to care whether the
provincial cavalry participated in campaigns. Instead, there was
an attempt to levy a special tax, called "*timar* substitute" (*bedel-i
timar*), on *timar* holders who either did not or were not asked to
show up for military duty. The reasoning was sound enough: a
timar was granted so the holder would perform military duties; if he
did not, for whatever reason, then he should pay instead. But the
fact that such a tax was even considered indicates how obsolete the
timar system had become.

The Rise of the *Beylerbeyi*

While the *timar* holders were neglected or even taxed, the *ümerā*
were supported to a certain extent. This support, however, was not
uniform; it tended to benefit the *beylerbeyi* rather than the *sancakbeyi*.
This, too, is connected with the weakening of the *dirlik* system. We
have seen that the *sancakbeyi* was primarily involved with the
supervision of *dirlik* holders in his district, and as the *timar*-holding
cavalry lost its military effectiveness the *sancakbeyi*, the immediate
commander, was also reduced in stature.

We have noted that already in the 1580s the *sancakbeyi* were
left out of office for ever longer periods. Paradoxically, just as the
ümerā were experiencing financial difficulties, they came under
political pressure to maintain larger households, as can be inferred
from the seventeenth-century appointment registers, which, while

omitting *hās* figures, supplied instead information deemed more relevant under the new conditions. When there were more candidates than posts, *why* a certain official was appointed is indicated in many entries. Because patronage relations had become much more important, for example, some entries note who proposed the candidate for office.[30] The notation "because he has a well-fitted out household" (*kapısı mükemmel olduğundan*) is given as the reason for appointment in some other cases, involving both reappointments after a period out of office and promotions to *sancakbeyi* rank.[31] The indication is that *beys* who were able to maintain larger households were preferred for promotion and advancement, and also had shorter periods out of office.[32] A vicious circle ensued: *beys* in office longer were in a better position to maintain retinues and were therefore preferred in appointments. Keeping a large household, originally a duty to the state, became a political necessity in the fierce competition for office.

The sad story of a certain *sancakbeyi* deserves mention here, not so much because it is representative, but because it indicates the extent of the troubles that could afflict one who fell behind in the competition. We learn of Ömer Bey's case because he died leaving some property but more debts, and in the estate register of Edirne, where his home was, the circumstances of his death and the nature of his debts are noted in some detail.[33] Ömer Bey took part in the Austrian campaign in 1601. Apparently he was out of office at the time for he was forced to borrow 89,660 *akçes* from his sister to pay his household expenses. Having served in the campaigns for three years he was rewarded with a *sancak* appointment in 1604. But, when he went to assume command of his *sancak* he was unable to do so for an unspecified reason: perhaps someone else was appointed to the same post at the same time—disputes between *beys* both of whom held valid appointment certificates were not uncommon in those especially chaotic times. The following year he was appointed *sancakbeyi* of Teke in southern Anatolia and he went there with his son and his retinue to take command. The previous governor of Teke, however, refused to give up the *sancak* and the two *beys* clashed; Ömer Bey's retinue was routed and he and his son were killed in an ambush. By that time the unfortunate Ömer Bey had borrowed a total of 255,830 *akçes* from his sister and more from other sources. After his property with a value of 137,000 *akçes* was sold, unpaid debts still amounted to about 150,000 *akçes*.

This episode took place while the Austrian war was still raging and the Celāli revolts in Anatolia had reached a peak. Conditions were quite confused until peace was signed with Austria in 1606 and the Celālis were suppressed in 1609. Ömer Bey's case, then, is an extreme one in unusual circumstances. But, even after a degree of stability returned, the competition for office remained a fact of life, if not as ruthless as during the "time of troubles" at the turn of the century.

While the *sancakbeyi* were left, by and large, to their own devices, a further change occurred in provincial administration in the 1630s to augment the revenues of *beylerbeyi*s, especially in frontier provinces. Governors appointed to Özü (northwestern Black Sea coast), Trabzon, and Van were given, besides the usual revenues, *sancak*s as "additions" (*zamīme*), sometimes in their own province but sometimes elsewhere. In certain other frontier provinces *sancak*s were abolished completely to be added to the governor's *hās*: Bihke in Bosnia, Semendire in Budin, Sigetvar in Kanije, Filek in Egri, and Bayburd in Erzurum all lost their *sancak* status in the 1630s.[34] Clearly, the *sancak* had lost its position as the primary administrative unit in the empire with the decline of the *timar* system. It was not even important to maintain a district as *sancak*; the primary consideration was to support the *beylerbeyi* of the province. *Sancak*s as *arpalık*, as *zamīme*, or simply incorporated in the *beylerbeyi hās* increased areas under the authority of an "absentee" governor.

In addition to receiving the lion's share of government support, the *beylerbeyi* also resorted to increased exactions from the subjects. Just as the sultan regularized *avārız* taxes to increase his household, so the *ümerā* invented extra-legal taxes to increase theirs. In the course of the sixteenth century the government attempted to put an end to such forcible collections from the *reāyā*,[35] but, especially during the Celāli revolts, officers of the state were allowed a free hand in order to be able to combat the rebels. So much so that a modern historian comments:

tax collection and banditry collapse into the same undifferentiated activity of living off the land, so that whether or not a man is a rebel comes to depend less on what he does than on the more or less fortuitous fact that he has or has not an official authorization for his maraudings.[36]

This comment refers to the extraordinary conditions of the period around 1600. But later on, too, *beylerbeyi*s continued to harass the *reāyā* while the government looked away. An episode related by Naīmā, the seventeenth-century historian, is particularly instructive in this context. In the early 1630s a certain İlyas Paşa was considered a rebel against the state specifically because he oppressed the *reāyā*. A government force, under the command of Küçük Ahmed Paşa, captured him after an extended struggle and brought him to the sultan, Murad IV. The sultan had İlyas Paşa executed immediately, then turned his wrath on Küçük Ahmed Paşa and accused him of illegal exactions as well. Ahmed Paşa was terrified that he too would lose his head. He did not deny the charge but defended himself by saying that he had also spent his own money, even borrowed some funds, to be able to perform the task entrusted to him. Murad IV talked at length on the importance of avoiding oppression and treating the *reāyā* well, but in the end rewarded Ahmed Paşa with a robe of honor and an important appointment![37] The main thing was that *paşa*s loyal to the sultan should have the funds to perform their duties; if, in the meantime, the subjects had to pay more than the regular taxes, this was reprehensible but unavoidable.

We have few documents that show the official revenues of *beylerbeyi*s in the seventeenth century, but all the cases that have come to light indicate that *beylerbeyi* revenues had increased enormously compared to their sixteenth-century equivalents. A register on the annual accounting of Öküz Ömer Paşa, governor of Diyarbekir, gives his official revenues as 120,000 *kuruş* for a one-year period in 1670–71.[38] This is six times higher than the 20,000 *kuruş* (1,200,000 *akçe*s; 60 *akçe*s per *kuruş*) reported as the standard *hās* of a Diyarbekir *beylerbeyi* in the sixteenth century. In Egypt, too, the governor's official income went up, in 1671, from about 5–6 million *akçe*s to about 24 million *akçe*s.[39] The revenues of the central government also went up from the sixteenth to the seventeenth century but by only about 25 percent.[40] Even when the inflation is taken into account, it is clear that some *beylerbeyi*s, at least, not only preserved their income level, but increased it two- or threefold— much more than the central treasury was able to increase its revenues. The indication is that the *beylerbeyi* increased their power and wealth not only within the provincial administration, at the expense of lower-ranking officials, but also vis-à-vis the central government.

The examples we have seen concern official revenues only. In addition the *ümerā* also had incomes from their economic activities. A vezir famous for his entrepreneurial ability was Derviş Mehmed Paşa (d. 1655), who provided millions of *akçe*s to his agents to engage in international trade. Naīmā writes extensively on the *paşa*'s activities, not necessarily because he was unique but because he put forward ideas on the subject. The *paşa* argued that the only way an official could maintain a large household and perform his duties without oppressing the *reāyā* was through economic invest-ments. This went against classical Ottoman political doctrine, which required a clear distinction among administrators, culti-vators, artisans, and merchants. In the context of the seventeenth century, Derviş Mehmed Paşa was justified by Naīmā.[41]

Very often the seventeenth-century *beylerbeyi*, in addition to his traditional duties, was also the "overseer of revenues" (*nāzır-ı emvāl*) of his province. As such he was placed above all financial officials (*defterdār*) sent from Istanbul, other revenue collectors, and tax farmers. How lucrative such a position was is indicated by a complaint of Gelibolulu Mustafa Āli, a high-level bureaucrat, historian, and social critic. Āli wrote that governors of Bagdad were willing to pay the central government 40,000 gold pieces to be appointed as *nāzır* while their salary would be only 30,000 gold pieces; Āli accused them of keeping for themselves more than twice what they remitted to Istanbul.[42].

The annual accounting of Öküz Ömer Paşa, governor of Diyarbekir in 1670–71 (but not a *nāzır*), itemized his revenues and expenditures, allowing a fairly detailed picture of the *paşa*'s activities.[43] For one thing, Ömer Paşa's income came from all parts of his province, showing that his men intervened in all *sancak*s. Furthermore, the governor received a fee from all appointments within the province: all *sancakbeyi*, all *dirlik* holders, all central army troops stationed in Diyarbekir, and all guild officials paid this fee, an excellent indication of the supreme power of the governor in his province. Among the expenditures the single largest item, more than a third of the total, was a remittance to Istanbul. Together with what the *paşa* spent on officials from the center, as well as remittances to his own agent (*kapı kethüdāsı*) in Istanbul, direct transfers to and expenses in his relations with the center accounted for almost half of the *paşa*'s total expenditures. In return for a sizeable remittance (*cāize*), then, the sultan was leaving the *paşa* in total command of all officials in the province. A governor who was also "overseer of revenues" obviously wielded even greater power in his domain.

The result was that by the mid-seventeenth century there had emerged in all corners of the empire *beylerbeyi* in control of vast economic resources, commanding huge retinues, each the size of a small army. The central government at first encouraged this development; may indeed have planned a relative shift in provincial administration, in conjunction with the decline of the *timar* system, from the *sancak* to the province as the main unit. But by mid-century the enormously powerful governors challenged the central government itself, in what is known in Ottoman historiography as the Abaza Hasan Paşa revolt (1658). It took all the energies of the state to suppress the revolt and establish a more stable relation with the governors thereafter. Nevertheless, the changes that had occurred since the sixteenth century were irreversible.

Recapitulation
and Conclusion

DURING THE CENTURY we have been studying and in the context of our theme three interrelated but distinct developments stand out: central government officials came to take over provincial administration positions at higher ranks; the province replaced the district as the main administrative unit; patronage relations and household affiliations became dominant factors in the polity.

These developments took place against the backdrop of the growing obsolescence of the provincial cavalry. As the classical system, based on apportioning *dirlik*s to cavalrymen and to their officers, became an unsatisfactory arrangement, experience in this career became irrelevant in terms of provincial administration. In the first half of the sixteenth century officers trained at the center, in the sultan's household, went out to join the *dirlik* system at fairly low or middle levels. There, competing with others already in the provinces, they hoped to reach *ümerā* ranks. Toward the end of the century, however, as there emerged a surplus of candidates for *sancakbeyi* posts, officers from the center were relatively more successful, even when they arrived without previous experience in lower ranks of provincial administration. Compared to a *zaīm* in the provinces they were better connected; but perhaps a more important reason for their relative success was the downgrading of the provincial career. This process continued into the seventeenth century when even the *sancakbeyi* rank fell into relative obscurity. By the 1630s palace and central government officials, even some directly out of the sultan's personal service in the *enderūn*, were appointed immediately as *beylerbeyi*.

The erosion in the status of the lower *ümerā* may appear to have reached even the *beylerbeyi* rank. Before 1550 the regular way to become a vezir of the imperial council and to move on to grand vezirate passed through the provinces. In the seventeenth century it became possible for a palace official to take office in central government, most typically as *yeniçeri* commander, and to go on to become grand vezir in one move. It would be misleading, however, to accept this as an indication of a diminution in *beylerbeyi* status. The governors general in the seventeenth century ruled in their provinces with much greater authority than in earlier times and with considerably increased revenues. The central government was now interested in direct cash contributions from the provinces, instead of alienating revenues at the source in support of an increasingly useless provincial army. Although this was done mainly through expanding tax farms at the expense of the *dirlik* system, the *beylerbeyi* now played an important part in the collection and transmission of state revenues. In some provinces he actually was titled "overseer of revenues" (*nāzır-ı emvāl*) in addition to his traditional role as governor (*vāli*). Even when he was not officially so named, he received contributions from all appointments in his province and sent on to Istanbul his own contribution.

The shift in provincial administration from the district to the province is also signalled by a change in the term used for province. A province used to be called a *beylerbeyilik* or a *vilāyet*. Both terms are too general to have any specific connotation: *beylerbeyilik* simply refers to the area that comes under a *beylerbeyi*, while *vilāyet*, a general term for administration, was applied to smaller units as well. From the 1580s the term *eyālet* came to replace the earlier terms. It is interesting to note that until then *eyālet* had been used for semi-autonomous areas. Kurdish *sancak*s, for example, which had special status, were termed *eyālet*s. It is not a coincidence that as the powers of the *beylerbeyi* grew, the area under his rule came to be called *eyālet*; the changing status of the province was thus indicated.

Along with the nature of provincial administration, the methods of recruitment and preparation of officers also changed. The most conspicuous change was the abandonment of the *devşirme* method of recruiting non-Muslim subjects for imperial service. It appears, however, that the importance of the disappearance of the *devşirme* has been exaggerated in Ottoman historiography: the *devşirme* method may have been dropped, but the essential feature of the *kul* system, training administrators in the imperial palace, was maintained. Slaves from outside the empire continued to be brought into the palace. The important change was that locally born Muslims were now taken into the *enderūn*, not simply as *müteferrika* in the *bīrūn*. The best-known example is Evliya Çelebi, the famous traveler: the son of a palace artisan, he was allowed into the *enderūn* after an encounter with the sultan. Another case, and an interesting one, is Silahtar Mustafa Paşa, the famous courtier of Murad IV: he was the son of a Bosnian merchant who came to Istanbul in his youth, was employed in several households, and finally entered the sultan's service.[1] Such Muslim-born *enderūn* pages were equally the sultan's *kuls*, his servants, if not slaves in the legal sense; their relations with the sultan and their public status seem to have been no different from that of sixteenth-century *kuls*.

The imperial household came to greater importance as its "graduates" left to occupy the highest positions in central and provincial administration. Competition for advancement now took place in the palace itself instead of at the lower ranks of administration. At the same time private households, those of prominent *ümerā*, also rose in importance. At the lowest level *reāyā* volunteers, who in the old days could take part in campaigns in the hope of receiving *timar* grants, now came to join *ümerā* households to change their status, as mercenaries if not as permanent members of the retinue. At the other end, *ümerā* household officials came to be appointed directly as *sancakbeyi* and even as *beylerbeyi*. Very often household officials served as interim governors in the name of their patrons, as their agents (*mütesellim*) taking command of a *sancak* or an *eyālet* until the governor himself arrived with the rest of his household. The fact that *enderūn* pages and *ümerā* household officials were directly appointed to *ümera* ranks does not, of course, imply that these were inexperienced men, simply that their train-

ing and experience was different from that of sixteenth-century
provincial officers.

Until recently it has been customary to speak in Ottoman
historiography of the "decline" of the empire from the late-
sixteenth century. I have been careful to avoid the term except in
the context of a particular institution. The *dirlik* system certainly
declined, but to talk of Ottoman decline from 1600 on, until the
empire's demise more than three centuries later in 1922, is to
overlook new arrangements that emerged in the second half of the
empire's existence. Perhaps the magnitude of the crisis around
1600 and the efforts of contemporary historians to understand its
nature have led to the fallacious notion of a long, monotonous, and
continuous decline. What is needed, instead, is a closer look at
changing patterns in more specific time periods.

I have tried to explain a particular process from 1550 to 1650,
a passage from the *dirlik* system of provincial administration to one
where the *beylerbeyi* supervised revenue collection in the provinces
and made cash contributions to the central treasury. In its essence
this was not a process of "decline"; it may even be referred to as
"modernization," in the sense that it was a shift from a "feudal"
arrangement to a monetary one. Furthermore, the shift was intended to increase the power of the central government, another
feature of the "modern" state.

The results, however, were not as intended. The classic *dirlik*
system, very different from feudalism, had been a highly bureaucratic one, controlled closely by a central government granting
dirliks for loyal service, routinely transferring *dirlik* holders from
one locality to another, and revoking grants when punishment was
indicated. The new arrangement in the seventeenth century, involving the increasing power of central government officials in the
provinces and greater cash resources at the disposal of the central
government, aimed at a greater degree of centralization. However,
the new *beylerbeyi*, supreme in their provinces, did sometimes challenge central authority. Even more important, the *beylerbeyi* came
to depend increasingly on the cooperation of local—and unofficial
—elites, either as agents (*mütesellim*) or as aides in revenue collection, thereby contributing to the rise of a powerful group of provin-

cial notables (*āyān*) in the eighteenth century. Such developments do not necessarily imply a general decline, but simply a greater degree of local leadership.

A quite different feature of the process we have been studying had much more significant consequences for the prosperity of Ottoman society in general. With the rise of households, both as a requirement of the state and as a political necessity in competition for office, a large part of the economic resources of the empire was tied to political struggles. Capital accumulation was largely intended for political aims, rather than for economic investments. This, more than anything else, determined the future course of Ottoman rivalry with Europe at the threshold of the industrial revolution and led to a decline of Ottoman fortunes relative to the increasing might of an industrialized and imperialistic Europe in the nineteenth century.

APPENDIX 1

Ottoman Provinces and Governors in 1527

LISTS OF OTTOMAN provinces in the sixteenth and seventeenth centuries are supplied in various types of archival registers, in the monographs of contemporary Ottoman authors, and in the accounts of contemporary writers, both Ottoman and foreign, who very often copied the lists from earlier documents or reports. Their accounts are, therefore, full of anachronisms and should be used with extreme caution. One of the most widely quoted sources, for example, is Ayni Ali's report, which contains not one but three separate lists of *sancak*s.[1] Ayni Ali's first list shows the *sancak*s in each *eyālet*; the second indicates the *hās* income normally allowed the *sancakbeyi* in each *sancak*; the third gives the number of *zeāmet* and *timar*s in each *sancak*. As the author himself states in his introduction, these lists were copied from registers of varying dates, and there are serious discrepancies among them. Although we know that Ayni Ali composed his report in 1609, we have no idea which periods his various lists refer to, except that they go back as much as thirty of forty years.[2] By comparing the lists with each other and also with archival registers we can infer that the oldest of his three lists is that which gives the *zeāmet* and *timar* figures and that the last, which is the listing of *sancak*s in each *eyālet*, must be quite close in date to 1609.

Of the seventeenth century *sancak* lists, the one contained in

Koçi Bey's report to İbrahim I (c.1640) appears to be copied from Ayni Ali's monograph. It is curious than even though Koçi Bey realized that the list did not reflect the situation in his day (he cites, for example, Özü as a separate *eyâlet* but does not mention its *sancak*s), he still was content to copy it, perhaps because he did not have access to the registers of the time.[3]

The list in Ali Çavuş's monograph on *timar*s, also, is closer to Ayni Ali's list than to the actual situation in his day (1653).[4] As for the figures Evliya Çelebi gives in the mid-seventeenth century as *hās* incomes of *sancak* governors, they are copied from the list in Ayni Ali's report, which in turn was taken from a still earlier register; thus Evliya Çelebi's figures are about a century off.[5]

Another mid-seventeenth century author, Katip Çelebi, mentions, with surprising nonchalance, that he obtained his lists from Ayni Ali and even from the mid-sixteenth-century writer Nişancı Celâlzade.[6] In short, after some scrutiny, only the list in *Münşeat üs-Selâtin* appears to be an authentic seventeenth-century source.[7]

Because of the inadequacy of these widely used reports, I would like to emphasize the need to refer to archival registers whenever possible; they form the source for the contemporary authors as well.[8] These registers are primarily of three types. Four lists at the Topkapı Palace Archives, undated but obviously all from the early years of the reign of Süleyman I (r. 1520–66), comprise the first type: they list all *sancak*s in existence at a particular date, with the names of the governors and incomes allotted to them. *Sancak* lists can also be extracted from the *ruznāme* registers in which are recorded, usually for a period of a few years, new appointments to and changes in *dirlik*s of all levels, from the *hās* of the *beylerbeyi* and the *sancakbeyi* to the smallest *timar*.[9] However, since only changes or new appointments are noted in the *ruznāme*, one cannot hope to end up with a complete list with any degree of certainty.

The appointment registers, which form the backbone of the present study, are the third type of archival registers that provide *sancak* lists. These registers are described in some detail in appendix 2; I will therefore refrain from discussing them here except to observe that they seem to be a fusion of the first two types, listing all the *sancak*s and recording the appointments to each *sancak* over a period of eight or nine years.

In view of the importance of relying on archival registers as much as possible, I have included here the facsimile, transcription, and translation of one of the Topkapı lists.[10] Before going on to this list itself, however, I would like to discuss all the lists in the Topkapı group and attempt to date them.

The earliest of the four Topkapı lists (TPA, D. 9772) has already been published in transcription by Ö. L. Barkan, who dates it September 1520–June 1522 (Şevval 927–Receb 928).[11] The portion of the second list on the Rumeli province, TPA, D. 10057, was cited by Gökbilgin when he published a register of all cities and towns in Rumeli (TPA, D. 9578).[12] The approximate date of this list can be established as follows: The Grand Vezir İbrahim Paşa appears in the list as *beylerbeyi* of Rumeli. We know that the governorship of Rumeli was bestowed on İbrahim Paşa when he was grand vezir in April 1526/Recep 932 on the occasion of the Mohacs campaign;[13] we also know that İbrahim Paşa relinquished this additional office sometime in the winter of 1526–27. I would guess that this list was prepared in late 1526, after the Mohacs campaign.

The third list (TPA, D. 5246), which is almost identical to the second in script, in composition, and in content, names a Kasım Paşa as the successor of İbrahim Paşa as Rumeli *beylerbeyi*.[14] Was the grand vezir also governor only for the duration of the campaign of 1526 or did he give up this post in the spring of 1527 when he crossed to Anatolia to suppress an uprising there? In any case, the last possible date for D. 10057, the spring of 1527, is also the earliest possible date for D. 5246. The last possible date for D. 5246 can be established with greater certainty: Sinan Bey, Koçi Bey, and Mustafa Bey, who appear in the list as governors of Alaiye, Amasya, and Karaman respectively, were killed during the Kalender uprising which was suppressed in June 1527/Ramazan 933.[15] The date of D. 5246 can thus be narrowed down to the spring of 1527.

The last list in the Topkapı series, D. 8303, is the most difficult to date primarily because it is the only list in the group where the chief *sancak* of each province, and consequently the *beylerbeyi*, is not mentioned; *beylerbeys*, of course, are easier to identify than *sancak-beys*. The best we can do is to say that the list dates from the late 1520s. The earliest possible date is 934/1527–28: Bâli Bey, who appears in earlier lists as the governor of İskenderiye (İşkodra), was executed in 934[16] and he is not mentioned in D. 8303. The last possible date can be established as 937/1530–31 since the list shows a Hüseyin Bey as governor of Alacahisar (Kruşevaç), whereas during the siege of Budin in 937 that post was held by an Ahmed Bey.[17]

It has been argued that the Topkapı lists should not be considered sufficient evidence for the administrative divisions of the empire because they do not exactly coincide with the land registers (*tahrīr*) of roughly the same period, that these lists should not be accepted as official documents but as private reports prepared for the reference of the imperial council or of the sultan himself.[18] It seems to me that the fact that the lists differ from the land registers is not sufficient reason to question their reliability. It is fairly obvious from a comparison of these lists with each other, as well as with other archival documents, that the Ottoman provincial organization was in a state of flux, especially in the first half of the sixteenth century when immense expanses of land were brought under Ottoman administration; the discrepancies merely reflect these changes.

Ottoman Provinces, Provincial Administrators, Incomes Allotted to Administrators in 1527 (TSA D. 5246)*

[On cover]   Detailed list of the districts
                    in the flourishing domains

                    He is the Clement Lord

The following is a detailed list of the names of the governors

* Province and district numbers added. First three entries translated in full, the rest in summary.

general and of the district governors in the [divinely] protected imperial domains in Rumeli, Anatolia, in the provinces of Karaman and Rûm, in the lands of Syria and Egypt, in Diyarbekir and Kürdistan, and in the province of Dulkadriyye, the livelihood granted to each by the exalted royal kindness, including the *yaya* and *müsellem* (auxiliary provincial troops) commands.

[The Province of Rumeli]

1. District of Paşa, in the name of the Governor General of Rumeli, the exalted Kasım Paşa.
2. District of Semendire, in the name of Hüsrev Bey, son of Ferhad Ağa, yield [of revenues] 500,000.
3. District of Bosnia, in the name of Mehmet Bey, son of Yahya Paşa, yield [of revenues] 605,000.
4. Gelibolu, Pulak Mehmet Bey, 605,000.
5. Niğbolu, Mehmet Bey of the Mihal family, 603,000.
6. Mora, the exalted Zeynel Paşa, 606,000.
7. Hersek, Ahmet Bey, brother of Mustafa Bey, 375,000.
8. Ohri, Hasan Bey, 300,000.
9. İskenderiye, Bâlî Bey, 605,000.
10. Silistre, Mehmet Bey, head palace gatekeeper, 540,000.
11. Avlonya, Süleyman Bey, 473,000.
12. Vilçitrin, Pîrî Bey, son of Balta, 406,300.
13. Alacahisar, Hüseyin Bey of the Evrenos family, 220,000.
14. Vidin, Yahşi Bey of the Mihal family, 400,000.
15. Yanya, Mehmet Bey, 600,000.
16. Tırhala, Hasan Bey, son of Ömer Bey, 512,000.
17. Prizrin, Bâlî Bey the Younger, 200,000.
18. Ağriboz, Ahmet Bey, son of Kasım Paşa, 320,000.
19. İlbasan, Hasan Bey, *Sekbanbaşı* (janissary officer), 200,000.
20. Vize, became a *hâs* (imperial demesne).
21. Köstendil, Mehmet Bey, son of Ahmed Ağa, 314,000.
22. İzvornik, Sinan Bey, Kethüdâ-ı Rumeli (Superintendent of the Rumeli fief register), 256,000.
23. Karlıeli, Kayıtbay, cavalier (*cundi*), 200,000.
24. Çirman, Ali Bey, *ağa-yı gurebâ-yı yemin* (commander of one of the household cavalry regiments), 152,000.
25. Kızılca müsellem, Mehmed Bey, son of Todor Mujak, 140,000.
26. Voynuk, Nebi Bey, superintendent of the royal stables, 80,000.
27. Çingâne, Ali Bey, son of İskender Paşa, 170,000.
28. Karadağ, İskender Bey, son of Çerni, 101,000.
29. Kefe, Mehmed Bey, nişanî (master of the imperial seal), 400,000.

30. Rodos and the [other] islands, Abdülcelil Bey of the İsfendiyar family, 300,000.
31. Selânik, [given out] as retirement pension.

Districts of the Province of Anatolia
1. Kütahya, the governor general of Anatolia, Behram Bey, 1,000,000.
2. Teke, İhtiyar Bey, 400,000.
3. Aydın, Lütfi Bey *emir-i alem* (palace official), 503,000.
4. Menteşa, Ferhad Bey, head wine steward, 450,000.
5. Saruhan, Mehmed Bey, 325,000.
6. Karesi, Mehmed Bey, son-in-law of Ayas Paşa, 200,000.
7. Biga, İbrahim Bey, son of Kurd Aydın Bey, 150,000.
8. Hamid, Sinan Bey, head tailor, 210,000.
9. Karahisar-ı Sahib, Okçu Sinan Bey, 300,000.
10. Ankara, Mehmed Bey, son of Pîrî Paşa, 364,300.
11. Kangırı, Mustafa Bey, 215,000.
12. Bolu, Musa Bey, son of Kızıl Ahmed, 405,000.
13. Kastamonu, Zağarcı Ahmed Bey, 250,000.
14. Sultanönü, in the hand of Kasım Bey, son of Şehsuvar Dülkadiri, as *zeāmet* (fief).
15. Hüdaverdigàr, *hās* (imperial demense).
16. Alaiye and Manavgat, Sinan Bey, brother of Yakub Ağa, 330,000.
17. Kocaeli, İbrahim Bey, son of Ömer Bey, 162,000.

Districts of the Province of Karaman
1. Konya, governor general Mahmud Bey, 700,000.
2. Kayseri [blank]
3. İçel, Sinan Bey, second equerry, 300,000.
4. Niğde, Mahzar Bâlî Bey, 230,000.
5. Beyşehir, Hasan Bey *el-çavuş* (herald), 150,000.
6. Aksaray, Hüseyin Bey, *ser silahdârân* (commander of one of the household cavalry regiments), 200,000.
7. Maraş, Üveys Bey, head equerry, 400,000.

Districts of the Province of Rûm
1. Sivas, governor general Yakub Bey, 700,000.
2. Amasya, Koçu Bey, 450,000.
3. Çorum, Sinan Bey, 153,000.
4. Canik, Sarrac Ali Bey, 150,000.
5. Karahisar-ı Şarkî, Mustafa Bey, son of Bıyıklı Mehmed Bey, 250,000.
6. Bayburd, İdris Bey, son of Ömer Bey, 305,000.

7. Kemah, Sinan Bey, 471,000.
8. Malatya, İskender Bey, son of Yularkısdı, 450,000.
9. Divriği and Darende, Mehmed Bey, son of Sinan Paşa, 188,000.
10. Gerger and Kâhta, Başıbüyük Mehmed Bey, 470,000.
11. Bozok, Mehmed Bey, son of Şükrullah Bey, 230,000.
12. Trabzon, İskender Bey, 500,000.

Districts of the Province of Şâm
1. Şâm, governor general Lütfi Bey, 1,000,000.
2. Adana, Pîrî Bey of the Ramazan family, 1,870,000.
3. Haleb, İsa Bey, son of İbrahim Paşa, 550,000.
4. Trablus, Haydar Bey, head taster (*zevvâk*), 400,000.
5. Kuds-i Şerif and Gazze, Üveys Bey, brother of Mehmed Bey, 550,000.
6. Hama and Hums, Mehmed Bey, son of Korkmas, 400,000.
7. Anteb, Mehmedşah Bey, 322,000.
8. Sis, Mahmud Bey, son of Davud Paşa, 180,000.
9. Tarsus, Hüseyin Bey, 150,000.
10. Nablus and Safed, Hacı Bey, 500,000.
11. Birecik, Mustafa Bey, son of Cerrah, 140,000.
12. Deyr and [sic] Rahba, Hüseyin Bey, 170,000.
13. Ekrad, İzzeddin Bey, 170,000.
14. Uzeyrili, Ahmed Bey of the Uzeyr family, 146,000.
15. Salt [and] Aclun, Iskender Bey, 200,000.

Districts of the Province of Egypt
1. Mısr (Cairo), governor general, Süleyman Bey, 4,000,000.
2. Commander of Mısr (Cairo), İskender Bey Horasani, 300,000.
3. Suyût, İsa Bey Köstendili, 250,000.
4. Cidde, as *emânet* (by a state controller).
5. Superintendent of revenues, Cânim (?), 400,000.

Districts of the Province of Diyarbekir
1. Amid and Mardin, governor general Hüsrev Bey, 2,500,000.
2. Harput, Gazi Kıran Bey, 400,000.
3. Arabkir, Levend Bey, 200,000.
4. Ruha, Mustafa Bey, 200,000.
5. Kiği, Mustafa Bey, 205,000.
6. Ergani, Mehmed Bey Menteşalu, 168,000.
7. Musul, Iskender Bey of the Arânid family, 338,000.
8. Anâ and Hit, Abdurrahman Bey, son of Öğünür Hacı Bey, 225,000.
9. Bire, imperial demense at the present.
10. Aşâir-i Ulus (Ulus tribes), imperial demense at the present.

Province of Kürdistan
1. Territory (*eyâlet*)* of Cezire, Mir Bedir Bahti.
2. Bitlis, Şeref Bey.
3. Hısnkeyf, Süleyman Bey, son of Melek Halil, holds [as] a district.
4. Siverek, Mir Seyyid Bey.
5. Mir Zahid, son of İzzeddin Şir.
6. Çemişkezek, Mir Hüseyin Bey.
7. İmadiye, Mir Hasan Bey.
   These [i.e., the above] are the great lords of Kürdistan.
8. Hizan, Davud Bey Hizâni.
9. Sason, Mehmed Bey Sasoni.
10. Palu, Çemşid Bey.
11. Çapakçur, Sultan Ahmed Bey.
12. Eğil, Murad Bey.
13. Sincar, Seydi Ahmed Bey.
14. Atak, Ahmed Bey.
15. Çermik, Şah Ali Bey.
16. Hayze, Mir Mehmed Bey.
17. Zerrik, Şahkulu Bey son of Mehmed Zerriki.

Müsellem Commands of Anatolia
1. Aydın, Saruhan, Menteşa, Sultanönü, Hüdavendigâr, Kocaeli, Karesi and Biga, *elliciyân* of Saruhan; Mehmedşah Bey, son of Şemsi Bey el-Fenârî, 58,000.
2. Bolu, Kastamonu, Ankara, Kangırı; Çadırcı Kasım, 66,000.
3. Kütahya, Karahisar-ı Sahib, Hamid; Hüseyin Bey, 65,000.
4. Teke and Manavgat, Çadırcı Ali, 45,000.

Yaya (provincial infantry) Commands
1. Kütahya, Kasım, *ser zağarcıyan* (janissary officer), 45,900.
2. Karahisar-ı Sahib, Hüseyin head carriageman, 50,000.
3. Karesi, Mustafa, *ser sasoncıyan* (janissary officer), 45,000.
4. Saruhan, Mustafa, ağa-ı Istanbul (janissary officer).
5. Biga, Kasım, *ser piyadegân* (janissary officer), 35,000.
6. Menteşâ, Ali *ser turnacıyan* (janissary officer), 45,000.
7. Hamid, Süleyman, 50,000.
8. Bolu, İlyas, *ser turnacıyan* (janissary officer), 40,000.
9. Aydın, Hüseyin, *ser solak* (palace official), 85,000.
10. Hüdavendigâr, Yusuf, 40,000.
11. Ankara, Yusuf, *ser piyade* (janissary officer), 45,000.
12. Sultanönü, Mehmed, 35,000.

---

* All subdivisions of Kürdistan are termed *eyâlet* as opposed to *liva*/district elsewhere. I use the term "territory" to convey the sense of being not quite part of the general system and of a degree of automony.

Figures 1–8. Ottoman Provinces, Administrators, and Incomes in 1527
(TSA D. 5246)

Figure 1. Opening statement and province of Rumeli.

Figure 2. Province of Rumeli (*cont.*) and districts of province of Anatolia.

Figure 3. Districts of province of Anatolia (*cont.*) and districts of province of Karaman.

Figure 4. Districts of province of Karaman (*cont.*) and districts of province of Rûm.

Figure 5. Districts of province of Şâm and districts of province of Egypt.

Figure 6. Districts of province of Diyarbekir and province of Kürdistan.

Figure 7. Province of Kürdistan (*cont.*) and *Müsellem* commands of Anatolia.

Figure 8. *Yaya* (provincial infantry) commands.

APPENDIX 2

Provincial Appointment Registers

THE PROVINCIAL APPOINTMENT registers, which form the major source of this study, are all to be found in the various classifications of the Başbakanlık Arşivi in Istanbul under the numbers MAD 563 (Maliye Defterleri-Financial Registers), KK 262 and 266 (Kamil Kepeci Collection), and Cev. Dah. 6095 (Cevdet Classification, Internal Affairs). Each register shows appointments to all provinces (*eyâlet*) and districts (*sancak*) of the empire during a period of eight to ten years. Of the four registers used in this study the last two are complementary (they cover the same period), so that we have data on three separate periods only. The periods covered are not significant in any particular way: they do not correspond to the reign of a sultan, for instance, or to the administration of a particular grand vezir. If either the beginning or the end of any register seems to correspond to any event this fact is noted in the descriptions below, but usually it is difficult to surmise why a particular register was started or abandoned at a particular time.

As I have indicated in appendix 1, the appointment registers can be viewed as a blend of lists showing *sancak*s and their incumbents at a particular date (the Topkapı group) and the *ruznāme* in which were recorded all changes of *dirlik*s of all sizes. One observation that supports this surmise is that the Topkapı lists and the *ruznāme* seem to have been abandoned after the appointment registers began to be kept; in other words, there are no surviving appointment registers which predate the other two types of documents. However, any attempt at determining the evolution of Ottoman bureaucratic practices on the basis of available documents must of necessity be tentative. MAD 563, which covers the period 1568–74, is the earliest appointment register I have been able to discover, but there may have been earlier ones. Furthermore, MAD 563 itself is miscatalogued (see below); there may be other such mislabeled registers in the Ottoman archives. Finally, it must be admitted that since these three types of documents were kept for different purposes there is no reason why they should not have been prepared simultaneously.

It is surprising that we have only four appointment registers extant from the sixteenth and seventeenth centuries. One would think that they would have been kept on a regular basis after they had emerged as a new type of register, presumably in the mid-sixteenth century; there should have been at least a dozen appointment registers from the period covered in this study. Their presumed loss may be explained by the fact that it is in precisely this period, from about 1570 on, that the sultan was less involved in the business of government. The appointment registers may have remained with the grand vezirs and perished with the vezirs' private papers. It is significant in this context that the only seventeenth-century registers we have are from the later reign of Murad IV, during the time this forceful sultan actively took matters in hand. (Since I have not combed the catalogues for later periods, I cannot tell whether the practice of keeping provincial appointment registers was continued after the seventeenth century).

To give a better idea of the information usually contained in these registers and how they differ from one another I have provided below sample entries from each register. It will be noted readily that the first register (MAD 563) contains much fuller information, while in the last two (KK 266 and Cev. Dah. 6095) the *hās* allotted to the *sancakbeyi* is completely left out and even such a standard item as the post an appointee held previously is frequently omitted. On the other hand, in the last period new items of information, such as the sponsor of certain appointees, begin to appear. One major difference between the registers is in the recording of appointments to lesser provincial officers. In the earliest register such appointments, i.e., to the posts of *müsellem* and *yaya beyi* in Anadolu province, as well as *hazine defterdarı*, *timar kethüdāsı*, and *timar defterdārı* in each province, are recorded regularly. In the second register (KK 262) the *müsellem* and *yaya beyi* posts are omitted altogether, and although the titles have been entered for offices, indeed for many offices not in MAD 563, such as "Kapudanlık-ı Fārisān der Bosna" (p. 10), "Kapudanlık-ı Mohaç" (p. 26), and "Ağalık-ı Azebān" in many frontier provinces, actual appointments are seldom recorded. Even the titles of the three main lesser provincial offices (i.e., *hazine-*or, in this period *maliye- defterdārı*, *timar kethüdāsı*, *timar defterdārı*) are not entered with any regularity in the last two registers; no appointments to these offices are recorded. This growing indifference to the lesser provincial offices no doubt parallels, and is further evidence of, their decline in status.

Sample Pages (with entry numbers added)

MAD 563 (s. 72)
Liva-i Kocaili
1. Der Tasarruf-u Bali Bey, mir-i sābık-ı Rodos. Fi 9 Recep sene 974. Hāsıl 236,526 [figures in *siyākat* script]. Berāt şüd maa terakki ve ziyāde fi sene-i m [ezbūr].
   [Undated note:] Mezkūr sancak Cezāyir Beylerbeyliğine ilhak olunmak buyuruldu.
   [Later entries above the line]
2. Der dest-i Kaya Bey, mir-i sābık-ı Sakız. Fi 27 Zilhicce sene 975. Hāsıl 250,000.
3. Der dest-i Ahmed Bey, mir-i sābık-ı Rodos. Fi 29 Cemāzi ül-ahir sene 979. Hāsıl maa terakki 260,000. Berāt şüd fi sene-i m [ezbūr,] bā noksan.
4. Der dest-i Haydar Bey, mir-i sābık-ı Azak. Fi 19 Ramazan el-mübārek sene 979. Hāsıl 275,590. Hāsıl maa terakki 400,000. Berāt şüd fi sene 980, bā noksan.
5. Der dest-i Mehmed Bey, an rüesā-ı kadırgahā-ı hassa. Fi gurre-i Muharrem el-harām sene 981. Hāsıl 260,000. Berāt şüd fi sene-i m [ezbūr].

MAD 563 (p. 72)

District of Kocaili (İzmit/Nicomedia)

1. In the possession of Bāli Bey, former governor of Rodos (Rhodes). Appointed on the 9th Receb, 974. Revenues 236,562 [figures in *siyākat* script; *akçes*]. *Berāt* (diploma of office) issued, with raise and surplus, in the same year.
   [Undated note:] This district has been ordered to be appended to *Cezāir* province [i.e., *Cezāir-i Bahr-i sefid*/Aegean islands].
   [Later entries above the line]
2. In the hand of Kaya Bey, former governor of Sakız [Chios]. On 27th Zilhice, 975. Revenues 250,000.
3. In the hand of Ahmed Bey, former governor of Rhodes. On 29th Cemāzi ül-ahir, 979. Revenues, with raise, 260,000. *Berāt* issued in the same year; with deficit.
4. In the hand of Haydar Bey, former governor of Azak [Azov]. On the 19th Ramazan the blessed, 979. Revenues 275,590. Revenues, with raise, 400,000. *Berāt* issued in the year 980; with deficit.
5. In the hand of Mehmed Bey, of the captains of imperial vessels. On the first of Muharrem the sacred, 981. Revenues 260,000. *Berāt* issued in the same year.

KK 262 (s. 25)

Liva-ı Peçuy

1. Sābıkā ikiyüz ondokuzbin akçe hāslar ile Dukagin sancakbeyi olan İsa Bey'e sene 982 Rebi ül-evvelinin dokuzuncu gününde hāsları bedeliyle tevcih olunup bādehū otuzbirbin akçe ziyādesiyle cümle ikiyüz elli bin akçe ile berāt eyledi. Fi 29 Cemāzi el-Ahir sene 984.
2. Sābıkā 200,000 akçe hāslar ile Kabur beyi olan Gazanfer Bey'e 989 Muharreminin 29. gününden livā-ı mezbūr ināyet buyurulup berāt eyledi, 240,000 akçe ile, fi 4 şaban el-muazzam sene 989.
3. Sābıkā Yanova beyi olan Mahmud Bey'e livā-ı Peçuy 210,000 akçe ile ināyet buyurulup 990 Rebi ül-evvelinin 15. gününden sadaka olunup berāt eyledi, terakkisiyle 237,700 akçe ile, fi gurre-i Cemāzi el-ahir sene 990.
4. Yanova beyi Gazanfer Bey'e verilmişdir. Fi 27 Cemāzi ül-ahir sene [9]92.
5. Zikr olunan Peçuy sancağı Piyāle Bey'den alınıp hatt-ı humāyūn ile sabıka İzvornik beyi olan Ömer Bey'e verildi. Fi 13 Şevvāl sene 993.
6. Şimontorna beyi [blank] Bey'e verildi. Bā hatt. fi 12 M[uharrem] sene [9]95.

KK 262 (p. 25)
District of Peçuy

1. Conferred on İsa Bey, formerly governor of Dukagin with revenues of 219,000 *akçe*, on the 9th Rebi ül-evvel, 982 with equivalent revenues. Later received a *berāt* totaling 250,000 *akçe* with a surplus of 31,000 *akçe*; on 29 Cemāzi ül-ahir, 984.

2. Graciously granted to Gazanfer Bey, formerly governor of Kabur with revenues of 200,000 *akçe*; from the 29th Muharrem, 989; for which he received a *berāt* on 4 Şaban the great, 989, with 240,000 *akçe*.

3. The district of Peçuy was graciously granted to Mahmud Bey formerly governor of Yanova, with 210,000 *akçe*; bestowed on him from 15th Rebi ül-evvel, 990; received *berāt*, with raise, for 237,700 *akçe* on 1st Cemāzi ül-ahir 990.

4. Given to Gazanfer Bey, governor of Yanova; on 27th Cemāzi ül-ahir [9]92.

5. Said district of Peçuy was taken from Piyāle Bey and given to Ömer Bey, formerly governor of İzvornik; by imperial rescript; on 13th Şevval, 993.

6. Given to [blank] Bey, governor of Şimontorna; by imperial receipt; on 12 M[uharrem] [9]95.

Cev. Dah. 6095 (s. 27, bottom)
Liva-ı Prizrin

1. Der Tasarruf-u Hüseyin Bey. Fi 22 Rebi ül-evvel, sene 1041.

2. Delvine sancağıbeyi olan Divitdārzāde Mustafa Bey'e istibdal itmekle virilmişdir. Fi gurre-i Muharrem sene 1042.
[Later entries above the line]

3. Sabıka [blank] Sancağıbeyi olan Cafer'e virilmişdir. Bā ricā-ı ser bostancıyān-ı hāssa. Fi 15 Şaban sene 1042. Bā hatt-ı humāyūn.

4. Liva-ı mezbur alaybeyisi olan Osman's cānib-i humāyūndan virilmişdir. Fi gurre-i Muharrem sene 1045. Bā hatt.

Cev. Dah. 6095 (p. 27, bottom)
District of Prizrin

1. In the possession of Hüseyin Bey. Appointed on 22 Rebi ül-evvel 1041.

2. Given, by exchange, to Divitdārzāde Mustafa Bey, governor of Delvine. on 1st Muharrem 1042.
[Later entries above the line]

3. Given to Cafer, former governor of [blank]. By intercession of the commander of the imperial guards (lit., gardeners). On 15th Şaban 1042. By imperial rescript.

4. Given to Osman, alaybeyi (cavalry commander) of this district, by the imperial government (lit., from the side of the emperor). On the first of Muharrem 1045. By [imperial] rescript.

KK 266 (s. 26, top)
Liva-ı Prizrin
  1. Bilfiil Mustafa Bey üzerinde. Fi gurre-i Muharrem, sene 1042.
  2. Sābıkā [blank] sancağıbeyi olan Cafer'e verilmişdir. Bā ricā-i ser bostancıyān-ı hāssa. Fi 15 Şaban sene 1042.
  3. Prizrin alaybeyisi Osman Bey'e ordu-u humāyūn tarafından verilmeğin mucibince [?] zabtına der-i devletten dahi hükm-ü şerif verilmişdir. Fi 14 Cemāzi ül-ahir sene 1045.
  4. Sābıkā Hersek Sancakbeyi olan Deli Piri'ye verilmişdir, Fi 6 Şaban sene 1046. Bā hatt. Ali [? name of scribe].
  5. Bi-hāsıl olmağla mezkūr Deli Piri'ye Ohri sancağı verilüb liva-i mezbūr mahlūl olmağın sābıkā bu sancakdan māzūl Cafer Bey'e verilmişdir. Fi 8 Şevvāl sene 1047. Bā hatt-ı şerif.
     [Last entry above the line]
  6. Sābıkā Delvine sancağıbeyi olan Osman dāme mecduhuya veril-mişdir. Fi gurre-i Cemāzi ül-ahir sene [10]51. Bā hatt-ı humāyūn.

KK 266 (p. 26, top)
District of Prizrin
  1. At present on Mustafa Bey. Appointed on 1st Muharrem 1042.
  2. Given to Cafer, former governor of [blank]. By intercession of the commander of the imperial guards (lit., gardeners). On 15th Şaban 1042.
  3. Since it was given to Osman Bey the *alaybeyi* (cavalry com-mander) of Prizrin, by the imperial army [i.e., by the commander of the army, in this case the grand vezir]; an imperial order has been issued that he may accordingly take command [of the district]. On the 14th Cemāzi ül-ahir 1045.
  4. Given to Deli Piri, former governor of Hersek. On 6th Şaban 1046. By [imperial] rescript. Ali [? name of scribe].
  5. [This district] being unproductive [of revenues] the aforemen-tioned Deli Piri was given Ohri district; this district thus being vacant it was given to Cafer Bey, formerly governor of (lit., dismissed from) this district, on 8th Şevval 1047, by imperial rescript.
     [Last entry above the line]
  6. Given to Osman, may his glory endure, former governor of Delvine. On 1st Cemāzi ül-ahir [10]51. By imperial rescript.

Figures 9–12. Provincial Appointment Registers

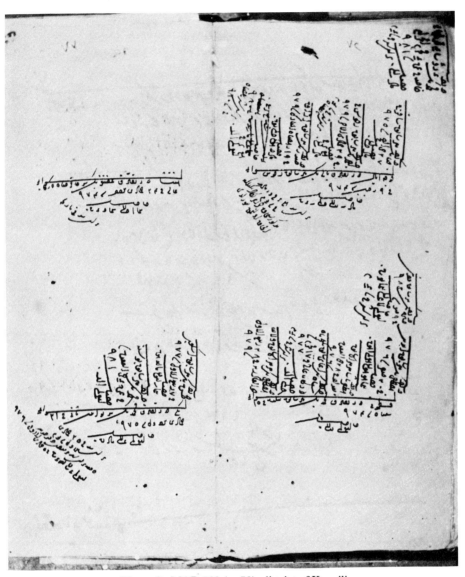

Figure 9. MAD 563 (p. 72), district of Kocaili.

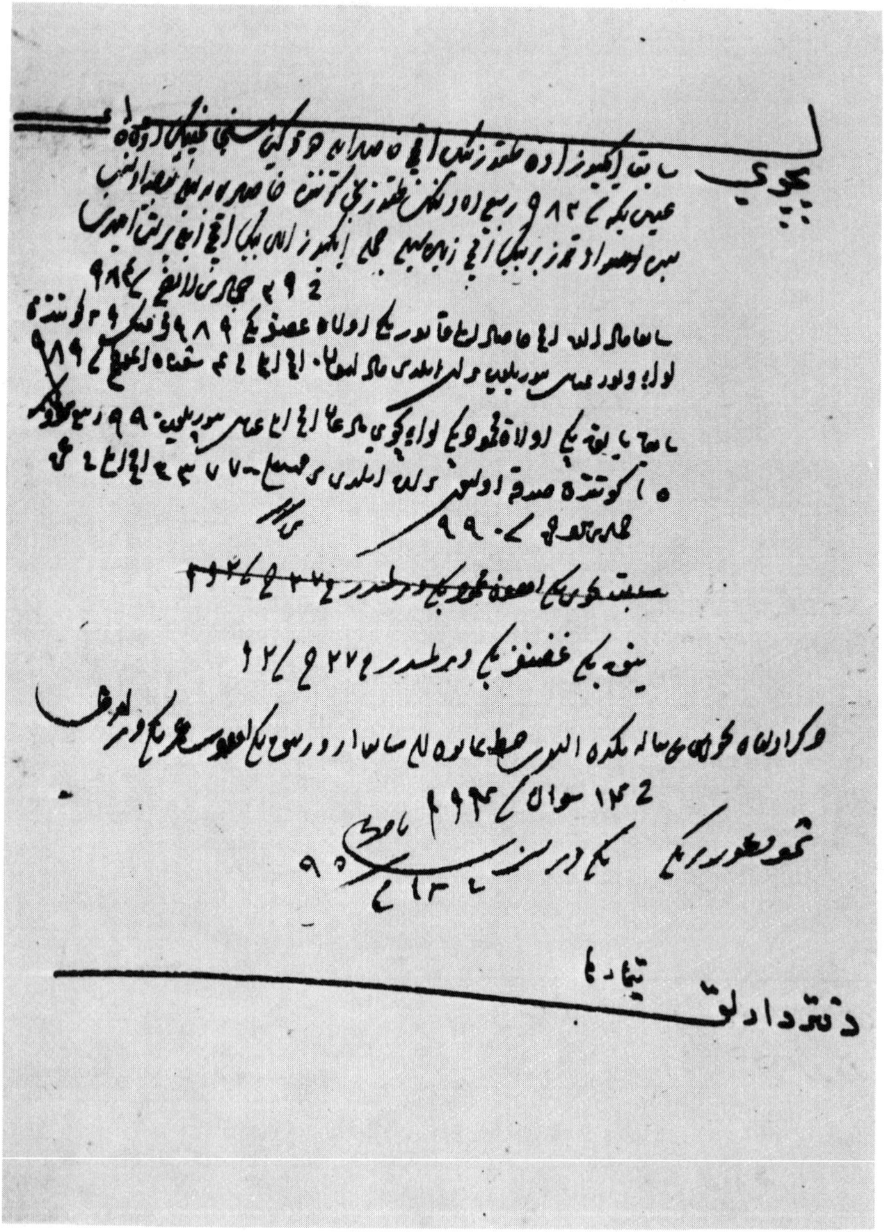

Figure 10. KK 262 (p. 25), district of Peçuy.

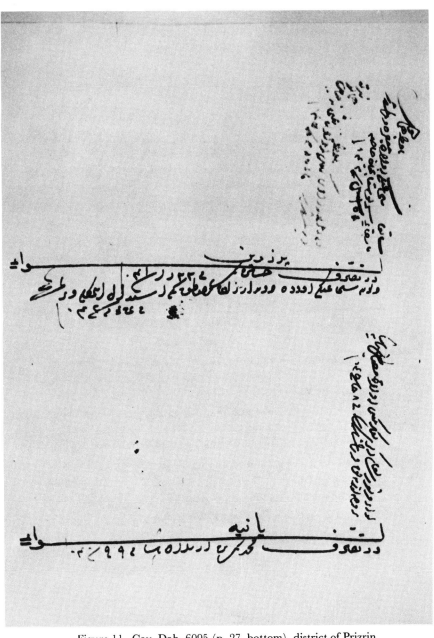

Figure 11. Cav. Dah. 6095 (p. 27, bottom), district of Prizrin.

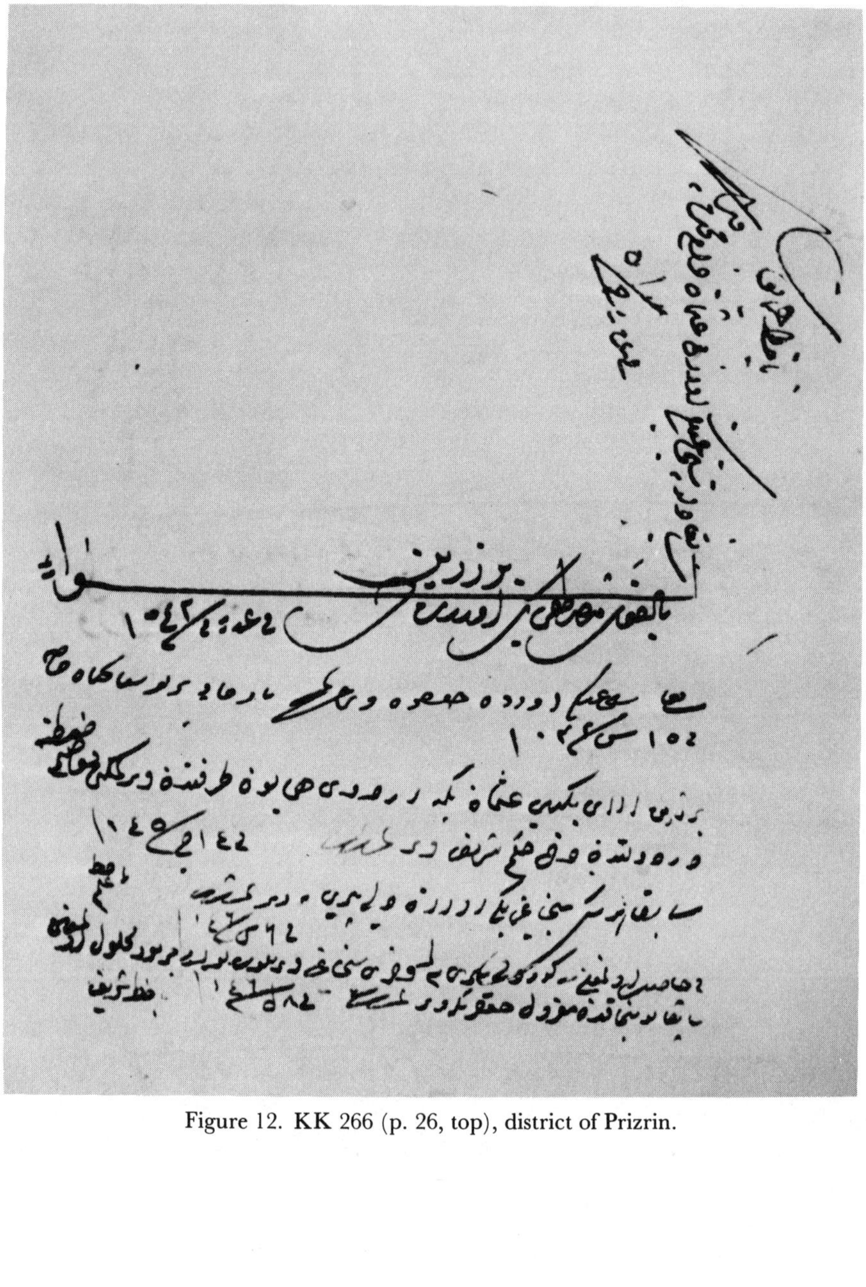

Figure 12. KK 266 (p. 26, top), district of Prizrin.

Descriptions

MAD 563 (1568–1574)

This register is described in the *Maliye Defterleri* catalogue as a *zeāmet* register. Indeed, the first thirty-six pages contain only *zeāmet* records, but the rest of the volume is comprised of provincial appointments. Evidently the register was at one point bound together with a *zeāmet* register of the same size and from the same period. In this hasty and careless binding many pages were out of order, some even placed upside down. The register was paginated after the material was thus bound incorrectly; the correct order should be as follows: 214–220, 37–76, 115–154, 174–155 (pages upside down), 77–114, 175–213. The bottom half of the last few pages of the register, from p. 206 on, is completely decayed and has been torn away. One or more sheets, which should have come between pages 220 and 37, have been lost.

Dating. The first appointment entry under each *sancak* indicates the incumbent at the time the register was first prepared. To determine the exact beginning of the register, therefore, I looked at the dates of the latest first appointment entries and the earliest second appointments. The latest first appointment dates are from mid Zilkāde 975 (May 1568): 15 Zilkāde for Gelibolu (p. 40) and Cezāir *timar kethüdāsı* (p. 44); 6 Zilkāde for Ağriboz (p. 41) and Vidin (p. 61); there are several other late first appointments from Ramazan 975 (March 1568). The earliest second entries are dated 26 Zilkāde 975: Ankara (p. 70) and Karahisar-ı Şarki (p. 147).

There are, however, two second entries which are *earlier* than the latest first entries: Erzurum *timar kethüdāsı*, 22 Ramazan (p. 170), and Karek and Şavbek, 5 Zilkāde (p. 157). One possible explanation is that while the register was prepared before Zilkāde 975, the Gelibolu, Cezair *timar kethüdāsı*, Ağrıboz, and Vidin posts were vacant then and the appointments were recorded when they were made a short time later. A less likely explanation is that although the register was prepared in Zilkāde 975, the appointments to Erzurum *timar kethüdāsı* and to Karek-Şavbek were so recent that the previous appointments were also recorded. The earliest possible data for the commencement of the register would be Ramazan 975 (March 1568) according to the first explanation, and Zilkāde 975 (May 1568) a according to the second; definitely the spring of 1568 in either case.

Of course, there are much earlier first entries, such as Tercil (p. 83) in Diyarbekir province, 28 Rebi ül-ahir 959; and under Soğman (p. 150) and Mazgird (p. 151), both in Erzurum province, 2 Ramazan 960 and 13 Şaban 958 respectively. These dates are of no importance for our purpose here since they merely indicate that some incumbents at the time the register was first prepared had been at their posts for a long time.

The end date of MAD 563 is easier to determine. All last entries date from early 982 (late summer 1574): 20 Rebi ül-ahir for Sirem (p. 51) and Fülek (p. 53), 1 Cemāzi ül-evvel for *liva-ı piyādegān-ı Karasi* (p. 126), 28 Cemāzi ül-evvel for Akkirman (p. 218). Sultan Selim II died on 1 Ramazan 982/15 December 1574, just two months after this last date; we can guess that there were no new appointments during those two months and that the register was abandoned at the end of his reign.

KK 262 (1578–1599)

This register is in generally good condition, though some sections are misbound: pp. 266–69 should come between pages 8 and 9; pp. 122–25 form a later addition which should have come after p. 129. A list, numbered pp. 90–91, is also a later addition; it should have been placed following p. 86. The later sections of the register, from p. 217 to the end (p. 285), are later additions, mostly as a result of conquests in the 1580s from the Safavis in the southern Caucasus and in Azerbeycan. These later additions were made in a quite haphazard fashion, with some repetitions. Indeed, the recordings in all portions, the original as well as the additional, are incomplete, not only in that some of the standard information, e.g., the dates of appointments and the income figures, is missing, but also because, more importantly, some appointments are altogether omitted.

The fact that some appointments were never entered can be

established through a scrutiny of the existing entries. For one thing, under many *sancak*s there are long intervals between successive appointments, as shown in the examples below:

a. Under Vize (p. 6) the first appointment is dated 1 Zilhice 984, the second, 27 Safer 993 with an interval of 9 years.
b. Köstendil (p. 7): first appointment on 7 Cemāzi ül-evvel 985, second on 26 Cemāzi ül-evvel 993; interval of 8 years.
c. Çirmen (p. 7): second appointment on 4 Ramazan 986, third on 18 Rebi ül-ahir 994; interval of 8 years.
d. Sakız (p. 15): first appointment on 1 Zilkade 984, second on 27 Cemāzi ül-evvel 992; interval of 8 years.
e. Kocaeli (p. 15): first appointment on 12 Muharrem 985, second on 5 Muharrem 995; interval of 10 years.
f. İstolni Belgrad (p. 19): second appointment in 984, third in 992; interval of 8 years.
g. Sultanönü (p. 42): first appointment in Muharrem 982, second in 993; interval of 11 years.

A *sancakbeyi* was never left at one post for such long periods, aside from *sancak*s with special status (*ocaklık, hükūmet*). In some other cases we can tell with certainty that some entries are missing. Consider the following cases:

a. Hızır Bey was appointed to Silistre (p. 4) on 24 Zilkade 986. In the following entry we read that Silistre was given on 13 Rebi ül-evvel 989 to Yakup Bey when *Mehmed Bey* was dismissed. Clearly Mehmed Bey's appointment should have been entered (similar cases under Prizrin, p. 6, İlbasan, p. 6; Semendire, p. 18).
b. The first entry under Suğla (p. 14) is dated 1 Rebi ül-evvel 991. However, it is mentioned that Mustafa Bey, who was appointed to İnebahtı (p. 13) in 986, and İbrahim Bey, who was appointed to Ağrıboz (p. 12) in 988, had previously been *sancakbeyi* in Suğla; they should have been entered under Suğla (similar cases under Pojega/Klis, pp. 19 and 34; Sakız/Teke, pp. 15 and 39; Dukagin/ Prizrin, pp. 266 and 6).
c. Hüseyin Bey was transferred from Hamid (p. 40) to Safed (p. 66) on 6 Rebi ül evvel 992, but the subsequent appointment to Hamid is on 13 Safer 994. Since it is very unlikely that Hamid was vacant for almost two years, there should have been one or more entries under Hamid between 992 and 994.
d. *Sancakbeyi*s in Çorum (p. 53) and Arabkir (p. 53) were confirmed (*mukarrer*) at these posts in 992 but the original appointments were not entered.

While we can thus establish that there were omissions, it is quite difficult to determine if these omissions occurred at particular times. In general, one can say that omissions are more common from 986–87 to 991–92.

Dating. Because of the omissions it is impossible to determine, using the method we employed for MAD 563, when exactly his register was started. There are some second appointments, as under Prizrin (p. 6) and İskenderiye (p. 4), dating from 985–86, but many more first appointments as under Nakşa (p. 16), İzvornik (p. 18), Üsküb (p. 8), from a later date. As for the end date in many *sancak*s (e.g., Niğbolu, p. 3, Kastamonu, p. 42; Ankara, p. 38, Estergon, p. 20; Sakız, p. 15), appointments were entered as late as 996. But in many other cases the last entry is dated 992 (e.g., Avlonya, p. 4; Budin, p. 18), 991 (Zaçesne, p. 267; Rodos, p. 13; Midilli, p. 13), or even earlier (989 in Karahisar-ı Sahib, p. 41; and Yanya, p. 5). Again, since it is unlikely that there were no appointments to these posts after these dates and before 996, there must have been omissions during the last years the register was in use.

There are some indications that this register was used concurrently with another which was taken on the eastern campaigns. Were such a register to be found, it is probable that the two would complement each other (as in the case of the last two registers, KK 266 and Cev. Dah, 6095, below).

Expressions used in the recording of certain entries support this speculation:

    a. Ohri, 19 Muharrem 995 (p. 3): "Girü Serdar tarafından İdris Bey'e verilmeğin kayıd olundu." (Entered since it was returned to İdris Bey by the field commander.)

    b. Silistre (p. 4): "Ali Bey'e verilmiştir. 28 Şaban 994. Serdar tarafından ahire verilmiş, yine Ali Bey'e buyuruldu. 5 Zilhicce 994." (Given to Ali Bey, 28 Şaban 994. Was given by the field commander to somebody else; bestowed again on Ali Bey, 5 Zilhicce 994.)

    c. Hamid, 17 Zilhicce 994 (p. 40): "Serdar tarafından ahire verilmiş, yine Mehmed Bey'e buyuruldu." (Given by the field commander to somebody else; bestowed again on Mehmed Bey.)

    d. Safed, 3 Zilhicce 992 (p. 66): "Vezir Zal Paşa oğlu Mehmed

Bey'e mukarrer, Serdar Ferhad Paşa mektubu mucibince."
(Given again to Mehmed Bay, son of Vezir Zal Paşa, in accordance with the letter of Field Commander Ferhad Paşa.)

e. Karesi, 22 Cemazi ül-evvel 988 (p. 40): Hüseyin Bey appointed "Serdar Sinan Paşa cānibinden" (by the Field Commander Sinan Paşa).

What these notes definitely indicate is that this register was kept in Istanbul while the field commanders of the eastern campaigns also effected some appointments, some subsequently accepted and some rejected by the sultan. We can therefore surmise that the register was first prepared on the occasion of the eastern campaigns, which started in early 986/1578, that it was used intermittently until 996/1588 when it was completely abandoned, and that the more complete records of appointments were entered in a register now missing, which was kept at the field headquarters.

KK 266 and Cev. Dah. 6095 (1632–1641)

While KK 266 is in good condition, Cev. Dah. 6095 is misbound, mispaginated, and missing some pages. The correct order of pages should be 27–34, 25–26, 35–54, 17–18, 3–4, 5–8, 15–16, 1–2, 9–14, 19–24.[1]

In trying to ascertain the beginning date for Cev. Dah. 6095, we note that the first entries with the latest dates occur under Kastamonu (p. 37) and under Divriği (p. 44) in early April 1632 (18 Ramazan and evāsıt-ı Ramazan 1041, respectively). There are two exceptions: the second entries under Amasya (p. 43) and Köy (p. 15) antedate these first entries. It can be argued that these exceptions are due to certain special circumstances attending the recording of appointments under these two *sancaks*: the person appointed to Amasya in the third entry was the same person named in the first entry. It seems the first appointment to Amasya after the register was started is recorded in the third entry, but the previous two appointments were also entered with the purpose of showing that this person had previously been *sancakbeyi* at Amasya. As for the second exception, the second entry under Köy is dated 6 Ramazan 1041, that is, just at the time the register was started; the previous incumbent may have been entered in addition to the new appointee because the change was so recent. Since the earliest second entry is dated 21 Ramazan 1041/12 April 1632 (under Karahisar-ı Sahib, p. 51), the beginning date can be established as the first half of April 1632.

Notes of place names accompanying several entries indicate that this register was taken on the eastern campaign the following year: Üsküdar is specified with third entry under İzvornik (p. 30), dated 15 Rebiül-ahir 1043/20 October 1633 as the place of recording; İznikmid under Ohri (p. 29), dated 22 Rebiül-ahir 1043/27 October 1633; Diyarbekir under Tekman (p. 15), dated 22 Zilhice 1043/19 June 1634. These places and dates correspond to Grand Vezir Tabanıyassı Mehmed Paşa's march toward the east in the winter of 1633–34. The latest last entries are all dated Receb 1046/December 1636 (under Kayseri, p. 41; Safed-Sayda-Beyrut, p. 46; Maarra, p. 49), a short time before the dismissal of Tabanıyassı (from the grand vezirate) on 7 Ramazan 1046/2 February 1637. It seems, therefore, that this register was used by Tabanıyassı during his tenure as grand vezir and was abandoned when Tabanıyassı was dismissed.

A note on the title page of KK 266 reads "Sefer-i humāyūna götürülen sancak kaydından ihrāc olunan sahīh suret-ı kayıttır; bununla amel olunmak buyuruldu" (Valid copy of the *sancak* register taken on the imperial campaign; ordered to be used [to record appointments] henceforth). Thus we can tell that KK 266 was a copy made from Cev. Dah. 6095, prepared to be kept in Istanbul when the other was taken on campaign. Its date of preparation can be established as between 15 Muharrem and 1 Safer 1042/2–18 August 1632, since the *sancakbey*s of İlbasan (p. 27), Saruhan (p. 50), Karahisar-ı Şarki (p. 88) and the *beylerbeyi*s of Karaman (p. 54) and Maraş (p. 60), all incumbents at the time the register was prepared, were appointed on 15 Muharrem, whereas the earliest second appointment, under Selanik (p. 29), is dated 1 Safer.

It is surprising that this copy was made in early August 1632, more than a year before the grand vezir actually set out on campaign in October 1633. It may be that in the summer of 1632 the campaign was expected to start much earlier, perhaps as early as the fall of 1632. If this is so, one can surmise that Murad IV and the grand vezir Tabanıyassı Mehmed Paşa decided to postpone the campaign for a year to be able to restore order at the capital first. Alternatively, it may be that a copy of the standard *sancak* register was made so that both the sultan and the grand vezir could have a copy at his disposal, not necessarily when one of them was away from Istanbul, and that the note, cited above on the title page of KK 266 was added later when the grand vezir left on campaign.

Appointments as late as in 1051/b. 12 April 1641 were recorded in KK 266. It appears, however, especially when checked against the grand vezir's copy, that at various times appointments were not entered at all. Different stages that can be discerned in the use of this register are listed as follows:

a. During the fourteen months between its preparation (August 1632) and the departure of the grand vezir (October 1633) some appointments were not recorded, perhaps because the campaign had been postponed and all appointments were entered in the original register.

b. During the period the grand vezir went on campaign until he was dismissed (February 1637), especially after the sultan joined him in Erzurum in June 1635, the entries in the two registers correspond fairly closely. Still some entries to be found in one are missing in the other.

c. KK 266 is abandoned after the sultan and the vezir parted in Diyarbekir in Cemazi ül-evvel 1045 (fall 1635). Since Cev. Dah. 6095 is also abandoned in the winter of 1636–37, we have no trace of any appointments made after his date. Perhaps a new register was prepared in February 1637 for use under the new grand vezir Bayram Paşa but such a register, if it ever existed, has not survived.

d. After the sultan set out on the Bagdad campaign in late 1047 (spring 1638), KK 266 was in use again, still with some omissions, until mid 1051, the latest entries being on 5 Ramazan 1051 (8 December 1641) under Malatya and Antep (both on p. 60), 18 Ramazan 1051 (21 December 1641) under Pojega (p. 40). This date is nearly two years after the death of Murad IV and the accession of İbrahim I. We cannot say why the register was abandoned then or whether a new register was prepared after that.

Method of Exploitation—Sampling

Seven provinces, namely Rumeli, Cezāir-i Bahr-i Sefīd, Budin, Anadolu, Rum, Haleb, and Erzurum, were chosen as the sample providing the basis for my analysis. They were chosen because they are all provinces where "standard" Ottoman provincial administration was more or less in effect; in other words, provinces where the *"sāliyāne"* system was applied or where local autonomy was greater were deliberately excluded. On the other hand, the sample includes provinces in the two general regions of "standard" administration, the Balkans and Anatolia. To be able to contrast conditions in the interior regions with the frontier areas, the border provinces of Budin, Erzurum, and Haleb were specifically included.

This sample was utilized for the first two period only. Because the registers of the third period are riddled with so many omissions, it was impossible to gather a significantly large *sancakbeyi* population on the basis of only seven provinces. Moreover, the *sancakbeyi* population available in these provinces was further reduced because some *sancaks*, which were part of the *eyālets* included in the sample in the earlier periods, had by 1630 been detached to some newly created provinces, such as Özü, composed of former *sancaks* of Rumeli province, and Eğri and Kanije, composed of former *sancaks* of Budin province. To be able to retain a large pool of *sancakbeyi*, therefore, it became necessary to include all "standard" provinces of the empire. I believe this change in the basis of comparison between the periods is not major enough to invalidate the analysis.

As the next step, the information on the appointments found in the registers under different *sancaks* was reorganized according to individuals. This was done by taking the last person under each *sancak* and tracing his career through his previous posts, which are mentioned in each entry. Having the information on appointments sorted out for persons rather than for *sancaks* was especially helpful in two ways: sometimes an item of information for a particular person, such as his father's name, is mentioned in only one of the entries involving him; by bringing together all entries on one person's career his identity is more accurately and completely established. The person cards allow greater accuracy, also, in determining length of tenure at a particular post and make it possible to discover whether any time was spent between appointments. For example, let us assume that an Ahmed Bey was appointed to *sancak* A on 5 Muharrem 976 and that the next appointment to the same *sancak* was on 10 Ramazan 978. By following Ahmed Bey's later career we may discover that he was appointed to *sancak* B on 10 Şaban 978, in which case *sancak* A turns out to have been vacant for a month, or on 10 Şevval 978, in which case it can be established that Ahmed Bey was out of office (*ma'zūl*) for one month. Obviously, the person cards were most helpful in the case of the last three registers where many appointments were not entered.

The person cards for each period were then alphabetized in two groups corresponding to the two general regions of Rumeli and Anatolia. (A *sancakbeyi* who was transferred from one region to another at any point in his career, a rare occurance, was included in the region where most of his appointments occurred.) Samples needed were draw from these alphabetized groups.

APPENDIX 3

Appointment of a Governor

Synopsis and Comments

THE REGISTER WHICH is the source for this appendix was the record of *dirlik* assignments kept by the scribes in the retinue of the governor general of the Rumeli province. It records action taken by the governor general's office, certificates issued, reports sent to Istanbul, and the gist of whatever decrees came from Istanbul.

F. 628a records that Murad Bey was initially appointed governor of Alacahisar district (Kruševaç in Macedonia) probably sometime in Ramazan 948. The exact date of his appointment cannot be determined; the dates mentioned in the text refer to various steps in the process of granting his revenues.

Murad Bey must have been governor of another district with total revenues of 220,000 *akçe*s, for he was granted a 30,000 *akçe*s raise, bringing his total *hās* in Alacahisar to 250,000 *akçe*s. The previous governor of Alacahisar, Ahmed Bey, must have held the district with revenues of 220,000 *akçe*s, for this is the amount (218,980 *akçe*s, actually) entered as the *hāshā-ı kadīm*, literally "old *hās*," which should be taken to mean the existing *hās*. The revenues from four towns, including of course the seat of the district, constituted 62.4 percent of the existing *hās*, the remainder supplied by sixteen villages in various subdistricts, governor's dues, and in-

SOURCE: MAD 34, register of *dirlik* grants in the Balkan provinces (*Rumeli ruznāmçesi*), for the years 948–49/1541–42.

cidental levies the governor received from the *timar* holders of two subdistricts. It is not clear why he did not receive the same dues and levies (*niyābet* and *bād-ı havā*) in other subdistricts as well.

Murad Bey held an appointment certificate (*tezkere*), and the fact that he received, for an unspecified reason, a raise of 30,000 *akçe*s was entered in Istanbul on the back of this certificate (see second note in top margin, f. 628a). He brought his certificate, with the notation on the back, to the office of the governor general. To make up the raise three *timar*s, the holders of which had recently died, and the revenues of a town held previously by Bāli Paşa (the governor general of Rumeli province) were added together, making a total of 33,200 *akçe*s. This figure was, of course, greater than the 30,000 *akçe*s increase to which he was entitled. But the existing *hās* of 218,980 *akçe*s was less than 220,000 *akçe*s, so the total of 252,180 exceeded what should have been his total income by 2,180 *akçe*s only. This surplus (*ziyāde*) of 2,180 represented an amount which could not have been taken out of the vacant *timar*s added to the existing *hās*. Such a slight surplus over the formal rounded figure was noted by the expression *maa ziyāde* (with surplus) in the diploma of office. If the revenues amounted to slightly less than the formal figure of the *hās*, the expression *bā noksan* (with deficit) was entered. (See examples in Appendix 4, Career Samples).

The governor general's office had to write to Istanbul for approval of this surplus (see first note in top margin, f. 628a). The surplus was approved on 30 Ramazan 948, and the additional revenues were entered in Murad Bey's name two weeks later, on 16 Şevval 948. The governor general reported the final situation to Istanbul on 26 Şevval. As the next and final step an imperial diploma of office (*berāt-ı humāyūn*) would be issued in Istanbul. If there had been no changes in the existing *hās*, the diploma of office could be issued very quickly, even on the same day the appointment was made. But sometimes the preparation of the *berāt* took longer, as in Murad Bey's case, where new revenues were added to the *hās*; in such cases it appears that appointment took effect immediately, before the *berāt* was issued (see appointment dates and *berāt* dates in Appendix 4, Career Samples).

A year passed. During the winter Hapsburg armies besieged Buda. Ottoman forces in the Balkan provinces were ordered to relieve the besieged city and they were able to repulse the Hapsburg forces after a battle just outside the city, across the Danube, near the suburb of Pest. We learn in the next section (ff. 708b–710a) that Murad Bey took part in the battle of Pest, served with distinction, and was rewarded with another raise of 30,000 *akçe*s. Murad Bey took the opportunity of this change in the level of his revenues to request a change in the composition of his existing *hās*. He submitted to the governor general that two villages included in his existing *hās*, with revenues of 11,704 and 1,641 *akçe*s respectively, were too far from the rest of his holdings and that this created problems in the collection of taxes in kind. The villagers had to keep their produce, waiting for the governor's men to come in order to ascertain total production and to take the governor's share. Transporting the produce levied by the governor to his own depots was also difficult.

The governor general found Murad Bey's request reasonable. The two villages were dropped and, in compensation Murad Bey received two *timar*s amounting to 12,050 *akçe*s. On the other hand, the four other *timar*s he received amounted to 32,337 *akçe*s, more than the 30,000 he was to receive. In the end his new *hās* amounted to 283,222 *akçe*s. Evidently the previous surplus of 2,180 *akçe*s was now deemed a legitimate part of his holdings, for the new surplus was computed to be 283,222 minus 282,180, not 280,000 *akçe*s. The scribe made an arithmetical error and came up with a 942 *akçe*s surplus instead of 1,042. On 28 Şaban 949 this was reported to Istanbul; the undated note in the top margin of f. 708b records that the surplus was approved. The new *berāt* was presumably issued soon thereafter.

It should be noted that the governor himself reported to the governor general's office the newly vacant *timar*s which could be added to his has. In some cases the previous holders had died; in three cases, however, the governor reported that the holders should be denied their *timar*s for they had shirked their military duties. The governor general had to approve such dismissals and presumably submit them for Istanbul's approval as well.

Initial Appointment (f. 628a)

[Notes in top margin]
Pāye-i serīr-i a'lāya arz olundu; 2,180 akçe ziyādesi buyuruldu, Fi selh-i Ramazan sene 948 (Submitted to the sublime threshhold; the 2,180 *akçe* surplus was approved. 30 Ramazan 948)
30,000 akçe terakkiye hükm virilmişdir; tezkeresinin zehrinde musadderdir (Ordered a 30,000 *akçe* raise; entered on the back of his appointment certificate)

[Main *hās* entry]
Hāshā-ı Murad Bey, mirliva-ı Alacahisar; an tahvil-i Ahmed Bey (The *hās* of Murad Bey, governor of Alacahisar [Kruşevaç in Macedonia, Rumeli province]; from Ahmed Bey [i.e., the previous governor of Alacahisar])

1. *Hāshā-ı kadīm* (existing *hās*)

Nefs-i (town of) *Alacahisar, maa niyābet* (including governor's dues)	60,000
Nefs-i (town of) اورکوب, *maa niyābet* (including governor's dues)	25,000
Nefs-i (town of) قفوجه, *maa niyābet* (including governor's dues)	33,000
Niyābet [*ve*] *bād-ı havā-ı timarhā-ı sipāhiyān-ı kaza-ı* بتروس (governor's dues and incidental levies from the *timar* holders of the subdistrict of)	2,500
Niyābet ve bād-ı havā-ı timarhā-ı sipāhiyān-ı nāhiye-i بولواه, fi sene (governor's dues and incidental levies from the *timar* holders of the subdistrict of . . . , yearly)	800
Karye-i (village of) کورنه يکونجه, *tābi-i* (in) ارکوب	5,434
Karye-i (village of) توقوبجه, *tābi-i m*[*ezbūr*] (in the same [subdistrict])	11,704
Karye-i (village of) ابولاهيق, *tābi-i m*[*ezbūr*] (in the same [subdistrict])	9,067
Karye-i (village of) فونجنوج, *nām-ı diğer* (also known as) صوسيج *tābi-i m*[*ezbūr*] (in the same [subdistrict])	4,107
Karye-i (village of) کيکونجه, *tābi-i m*[*ezbūr*] (in the same [subdistrict])	6,133
Karye-i (village of) ديار سيجه, *tābi-i* (in) دلبو صجه	4,673
Karye-i (village of) غروداش, *tābi-i m*[*ezbūr*] (in the same [subdistrict])	7,749
Voynugān-ı karye-i (*voynuk*s of the village of) دوليه برسبويجه, *tābi-i* (in) دلبو صجه	1,000
Nefs-i (town of) Kurşunlu	18,000
Karye-i (village of) ماحوفات, *tābi-i* (in) اورکوب	4,472

Karye-i (village of) قوجالى, *tābi-i m*[*ezbūr*] (in the same
[subdistrict])   5,273

Karye-i (village of) بودلايجه, *tābi-i m*[*ezbūr*] (in the same
[subdistrict]) *voynugān* (*voynuk*s)   6,581

Karye-i (village of) سومادىبوفجه, *tābi-i m*[*ezbūr*] (in the
same [subdistrict]) *voynugān* (*voynuk*s)   5,500

Karye-i (village of) نابجه انجادق, *tābi-i* (in) دلبو صجه,
voynugan (*voynuk*s)   2,000

Karye-i (village of) دوليه دره كوفجه, *tābi-i* (in) اوركوب,
voynugan (*voynuk*s)   2,377

Karye-i (village of) ناردىك, *tābi-i m*[*ezbūr*] (in the same
[subdistrict])   1,969

Hisse-i āhir-i karye-i (other share of the village of)
دابقه بان   1,641

YEKŪN (TOTAL)   218,980

2. *İlhāk ilā zālik ki bedel-i terakki-i müşārileyh. Fi 16 Şevval 948*
(Additions equal to [Murad Bey's] raise. On 16 Şevval 948)

Nefs-i (town of) براكين, *tābi-i* (in) بتروس; *an tahvīl-i*
(from) *Hazret-i Bāli Paşa*   5,000

Nāhiye-i (subdistrict of) دلبو صجه, *tābi-i liva-ı* (in the
district of) *Alacahisar: An tahvīl-i* (from) *Solak
Mustafa ki müteveffa şüde* (deceased)

Karye-i (village of) بتكور, *tābi-i* (in) دلبو صجه   8,500

Karye-i (village of) بوغونجه, *tābi-i m*[*ezbūr*] (in the same
[subdistrict])   5,000

Karye-i (village of) بره زه قو فجه, *tābi-i m*[*ezbūr*] (in the
same [subdistrict])   1,500

YEKŪN (TOTAL)   15,000

Nāhiye-i (subdistrict of) دلبوصجه, *tābi-i m*[*ezbūr*] (in the
same [district]):
An tahvīl-i (from) *Hızır Voyvoda ki müteveffa şüde*
(deceased)

Karye-i (village of) اينجر جالى, *tābi-i m*[*ezbūr*] (in the same
[subdistrict])   3,200

Karye-i (village of) مروسوحى, *tābi-i m*[*ezbūr*] (in the
same [subdistrict])   2,500

YEKŪN (TOTAL)   5,700

Nāhiye-i (subdistrict of) اوركوب, *tābi-i liva-ı m*[*ezbūr*]
(in the same district)

An tahvīl-i (from) *Hızır bin İskender ki müteveffā şüde*
(deceased)

Karye-i (village of) لورمه, *tābi-i m[ezbūr]* (in the same [subdistrict])	5,000
Karye-i (village of) سيردنه سفارجه, *nām-ı diğer* (also known as) ماكي	2,500
YEKŪN (Total)	7,500
EL-YEKŪN-U MÜLHAKĀT (Total of Additions)	33,200
HĀSHĀ MAA MÜLHAKĀT (*Hās* including Additions)	252,180

*Livā-ı mezbūr müşārileyh bendelerine 30,000 akçe terakki ile sadaka
olunmağın zikr olan timarlar müşārileyh bendelerinin terakkisinden bedel
ilhāk olunup kābil-i ifrāz olmayan 2,180 akçe ziyādesiyle tevcih olunup
berāt-ı humāyūn sadaka buyurulmak ricāsına südde-i saadete arz olundı.
Tahriren fī'i-yevm el-sādis ve'l-aşrin şehr-i Şevvāl el-mükerrem sene semān
ve erbain ve tis'amia.* (The said district being bestowed on the
[sultan's] aforementioned slave with a 30,000 *akçe* raise, the *timar*s
cited above, equal to the raise, were added [to the existing *hās*].
This was submitted to the threshhold of felicity with the petition
that the imperial diploma of office be granted with a surplus of
2,180 *akçe*s which cannot be separated. Written on 26 Şevval
948.)

A Raise in the Governor's Revenues
(ff. 708b–710a)

f. 708b [Note in top margin]
Ziyāde 900 buyuruldu (Surplus of 900 approved)
[The main *hās* entry]
Hāshā-ı Murad Bey, mirliva-ı Alacahisar; an tahvīl-i hod (The *hās* of Murad
Bey, governor of Alacahisar; from himself [i.e., not a new appointment,
merely a change in the amount of revenues])

1. *An hāshā-ı kadīm* (from the existing *hās*)	
Nefs-i (town of) *Alacahisar, maa niyābet* (including governor's dues)	60,000
Nefs-i (town of) اركوب, *maa niyābet* (including governor's dues)	25,000
Nefs-i (town of) تقوبجه, *maa niyābet* (including governor's dues)	33,000

Niyābet [*ve*] *bād-ı havā-i timarhā-ı sipāhiyān-i kaza-i*
بتروس (governor's dues and incidental levies
from the *timar* holders of the subdistrict of)   2,500
Niyābet [*ve*] *bād-ı havā-ı timarhā-ı sipāhiyān-i nāhiye-*
i بولوان (governor's dues and incidental levies
from the *timar* holders of the subdistrict of)   800
Karye-i (village of) كورنه بكو نيجه, *tābi-i* (in) اركوب   5,434
Karye-i (village of) ابو لا هيق, *tābi-i m*[*ezbūr*] (in
the same [subdistrict])   9,067
Karye-i (village of) نو حقوجه, *nām-ı diğer* (also
known as) صوسيج, *tābi-i m*[*ezbūr*] (in the same
[subdistrict])   4,107
Karye-i (village of) كيكو نجه, *tābi-i m*[*ezbūr*] (in
the same [subdistrict])   6,132 [sic]
Karye-i (village of) ديبار سقه, *tābi-i* (in) دلبو صجه   4,272 [sic]
Karye-i (village of) غروداش, *tābi-i m*[*ezbūr*] (in the
same [subdistrict])   7,749
Voynugān-ı karye-i (voynuks of the village of)
دوليه سر سفويجه, *tābi-i* (in) دلبو صجه   1,000
Nefs-i (town of) Kurşunlu   18,000
Karye-i (village of) ماحوفات, *tābi-i* (in) اوركوب   4,472
Karye-i (village of) قوجالى, *tābi-i m*[*ezbūr*] (in the
same [subdistrict]   5,273
Karye-i (village of) بودولايجه, *tābi-i m*[*ezbūr*] (in the
same [subdistrict]) *voynugān* (voynuks)   6,581
Karye-i (village of) سومارىبوفجه, *tābi-i m*[*ezbūr*] (in
the same [subdistrict]) *voynugān* (voynuks)   5,500
Karye-i (village of) نابجه انجلاده, *tābi-i* (in)
دلبو صجه, *voynugān* (voynuks)   2,000
Karye-i (village of) دوليه كوره كوفجه, *tābi-i* (in)
اوركوب, *voynugān* (voynuks)   2,377
Karye-i (village of) نارديك, *tābi-i m*[*ezbūr*] (in the
same [subdistrict])   1,969

YEKŪN (TOTAL)   205,335

Nāhiye-i (subdistrict of) دلبو صجه, *tābi-i liva-ı*
(in the district of) Alacahisar:
An tahvīl-i (from) Solak Mustafa ki müteveffā şüd
(deceased)
Karye-i (village of) بتكور, *tābi-i m*[*ezbūr*] (in the
same [subdistrict])   8,500
Karye-i (village of) بوغونجه, *tābi-i m*[*ezbūr*] (in
the same [subdistrict])   5,000

Karye-i (village of) بره زه قوفجه, *tābi-i m[ezbūr]*
(in the same [subdistrict]) 1,500

YEKŪN (TOTAL) 15,000

An tahvīl-i (from) *Hazret-i Bāli Paşa Nefs-i* (town
of) يراكين, *tābi-i* (in) بتروس 5,000
An-tahvīl-i (from) *Hızır Voyvoda ki müteveffā şüd*
(deceased) *Der nāhiye-i* (in the subdistrict of)
دلبو صجه
Karye-i (village of) اينجر جالى, *tābi-i m[ezbūr]* (in
the same [subdistrict]) 3,200
Karye-i (village of) مروسوحى, *tābi-i m[ezbūr]* (in
the same [subdistrict]) 2,500

YEKŪN (TOTAL) 5,700

An tahvīl-i (from) *Hızır bin İskender ki müteveffā şüd*
(deceased)
Karye-i (village of) لورمه, *tābi-i m[ezbūr]* (in the
same [subdistrict]) 5,000
Karye-i (village of) سيردنه سفارجه, *nam-ı diğer*
(also known as) ماكيه, *tābi-i m[ezbūr]* (in the
[same subdistrict]) 2,500

YEKŪN (TOTAL) 7,500
CEM'AN DER İFRĀZ AN HĀSHĀ-I
KADĪM
(Total from the existing *hās*) 238,835

f. 709a

2. *An tahvīl-i mezkūreyn an bedel-i ifrāz-ı karye-i* توقوبمجه *ve* بان دابله *an*
hāss-ı kadīm. An 20 Şaban el-muazzam sene 949 (From the two
[persons] cited [below], equal to the [yield] of the villages of
… and …, taken out from the existing *hās*. From 20 Şaban
949.)

Nāhiye-i (subdistrict of) *Alacahisar tābi-i liva-ı*
mezbūre (in the same district)
Timar-ı (of) *Hüseyin ki müteveffā şüd* (deceased).
Fi 20 Şaban el-muazzam sene 949.
Karye-i (village of) بنالوفجه, *tābi-i*
m[ezbūr] (in the same [subdistrict]) 3,520
Karye-i (village of) مانجه, *tābi-i* (in) دلبو صجه 2,218
Karye-i (village of) بودورو فجه, *tābi-i m[ezbūr]*
(in the same [subdistrict]) 812

Hisse an karye-i share in the village of)
دابلوريك (in) *tābi-i*, بره اغو بنيجه　　　　　　3,000

YEKŪN (TOTAL)　　　　　　9,550

Nāhiye-i (subdistrict of) دلبو صجه, *tābi-i liva-ı*
mezbūre (in the same district)
Timar-ı (of) *Vuk zimmi* (non-Muslim)
Karye-i (village of) درا سقو فجه, *tābi-i m[ezbūr]*
(in the same [subdistrict])　　　　　　2,500

YEKŪNAN BEDEL-İ İFRĀZ-I MİRLİVA
(Total [of Additions] Equal to [the
Portion] Given Up by the Governor)　　12,050

*Mezkūr içün sancağıbeyi Budun muhafazasında ve Peşte muharebesinde
bulunmayup müstahak-ı azl oldı deyu i'lām itmeğin müşārileyhin [i]
frāzından bedel hāslarına ilhāk olundı. Fi 20 Şaban el-muazzam sene
949.* (The governor has reported that the aforementioned [i.e.,
Vuk zimmi] did not attend the defense of Buda and the battle of
Pest and is therefore deserving of dismissal.
[His *timar*] has been added to the *hās* [of the governor], as compensation for what he [the governor] has given up. On 20
Şaban 949.)

3. *İlhāk ilā zālik berā-ı terakki-i muharebe-i Peşte ber muceb-i hükm-ü şerīf.
Fi 24 Şaban el-muazzam sene 949.* (Additions as raise for [atten-
dance at] the battle of Pest, in accordance with the imperial
order. On 24 Şaban 949.)

Nāhiye-i (subdistrict of) اورکوب *der liva-ı* (in the
district of) *Alacahisar*:
Timar-ı (of) *Mustafa ser-asker-i nahiye-i* (troop
commander of the district of) دلبو صجه *ki*
müteveffā şüd (deceased). *Fi't-tārih el-mezbūr* (on
the same date).
Karye-i (village of) استو يلجه, *tābi-i m[ezbūr]* (in
the same [subdistrict])　　　　　　4,060
Karye-i (village of) ديلفامى, *tābi-i m[ezbūr]* (in
the same [subdistrict])　　　　　　2,349
Voynugān-ı karye-i (*voynuk*s of the village of)
استويلجه　　　　　　1,150
Hisse an karye-i (share in the village of) حاستوار,
tābi-i (in) دلبو صجه　　　　　　999
Karye-i (village of) درا قصر فجه, *tābi-i* (in) اورکوب　　800

YEKŪN (TOTAL)　　　　　　11,358

f. 709b

Hāshā-ı Murad Bey mirliva-ı Alacahisar (The *hās* of
Murad Bey, governor of Alacahisar [con'd])
Nāhiye-i (subdistrict of) دلبو صجه, *tābi-i liva-ı*
mezbūre (in the same district)
Timar-ı (of) *Mustafa ki müteveffā şüd* (deceased).
Fi (on) *24 Şaban el-muazzam sene 949.*
Karye-i (village of) حوليه سنو رود, *tābi-i m[ezbūr]* (in
the same [subdistrict])   6,700
Manastır (monastery of) ارهابفك, *nezd-i karye-i*
(near the village of) بولار   200
                                                          _____
YEKŪN (Total)   6,900

Nāhiye-i (subdistrict of) اوركوب, *tābi-i liva-ı*
mezbūre (in the same district)
Timar-ı (of) *Uğurlu merdüm-ü Hüsrev Bey* (of
Hüsrev Bey's household) *ve* (and) *Ali bin*
Hasan.
Karye-i (village of) بو حمير, *tābi-i m[ezbūr]* (in the
same [subdistrict])   8,579
     Hisse-i (the share of) *Uğurlu*   6,579
     Hisse-i (the share of) *Ali*   2,000

Mezkūrān içün sancağıbeyi Budun muhafazasında ve Peşte muharebesinde
bulunmayub müstahak-ı azl oldılar deyu i'lām itmeğin müşārileyhe ilhāk
olundı. Fi 18 Şaban sene 949. (The governor has reported that the
[two] aforementioned [persons] did not attend the defense of
Buda and the battle of Pest and are therefore deserving of dismissal. [Their *timar*] has been added [to the *hās* of the governor].
On 18 Şaban 949.)

Nāhiye-i (subdistrict of) دلبو صجه, *tābi-i liva-ı*
mezbūre (in the same district):
Timar-ı (of) *Cafer*
   Karye-i (village of) كورنه درود ليه, *tābi-i* (in)
   دلبو صجه   3,923
   Karye-i (village of) فورنجى, *tābi-i m[ezbūr]* (in
   the same [subdistrict])   1,577
                                                          _____
YEKŪN (Total)   5,500

Mezkūr içün sancağıbeyi kara davar ecr içün gönderilüb ol zamandan beridir
gelmeyüb ve Peşte muharebesinde bulunmayub müstahak-ı azl oldı deyu i'lām
itmeğin müşārileyhe ilhak olundı. Fi 18 Şaban el-muazzam sene 949. (The
governor has reported that the aforementioned was sent for rent-

ing oxen, that he has not returned since then, that he did not attend the battle of Pest and is therefore deserving of dismissal. His *timar* has been added [to the *hās* of the governor]. On 18 Şaban 949.)

CEM'AN AN ERBĀB-I TIMAR (Total
from *Timar*-Holders)   32,337

EL-MECMŪ' MAA MÜLHAK (Grand
Total with Additions)   283,222

Müşārileyh Murad Bey Peşte muharebesinde yoldaşlıkda bulunmağın 252,180 ilhak hāsları üzerine 30,000 akçe terakki idesiz deyu hükm-ü şerīf vārid olub ve mumāileyhin kadīmi hāslarından اوركوب *nāhiyesinde 11,704 akçe yazar karye-i* توقو مجه *ve nāhiye-i mezbūrede 1,641 akçe yazar* داىله بان, *hāslarından baīd olub ta'şīr mahallinde vakti ile ta'şīr olunmayub ve ta'şīr oldukda dahi mahsūl sāir hāslarının mahsūli ile bir yere gelmekle asīr olmağın zikr olan karyelerden ferāgat idüb andan bedel* f. 710a *liva-ı mezbūrede Alacahisar nāhiyesinde//müteveffā Hüseyin tahvīlinden mahlūl olan 9,550 akçe yazar karyeler ve* دلبو صجه *nāhiyesinde kendü mektub[u] mūcebince Budun muhafazasında ve Peşte muharebesinde bulunmayub müstahak-ı azl olunan (sic for olan) Vuk nām zimmi tahvīlinden mahlūl olan 2,500 akçe yazar* درا سقو فجه *nām karye ve Peşte muharebesi terakkisinden bedel kendü mektub[u] mūcebince bazı müteveffā ve bazı dahi Budun muhafazasında bulunmayub müstahak-ı azl olanların timarlarından 32,337 akçe yazar karyeler mahlūl olmağın birikdirilüb cümle hāsları 283,222 akçelik olmak üzere defter-i hākāniye kayd olunub kābil-i ifrāz olmayan 942 akçe ziyādesiyle tevcih olunub berāt-ı humāyūn sadaka buyurulmak ricāsına tezkere-i bendegi birle ol āsitāne-i murad-bahşa arz olundı. Tahrīren fi'l-yevm el-sāmin aşrin Şaban sene 949.* (The aforementioned Murad Bey having served [with distinction] in the battle of Pest, an imperial order has arrived saying give him a raise of 30,000 *akçe* on top of his consolidated *hās* of 252,180. Also the aforementioned has given up two villages of his existing *hās*, the village of توقو مجه, with a registered yield of 11,704, in the subdistrict of اوركوب, and the village of داىله بان, with a registered yield of 1,641, in the same subdistrict, for [these two villages] are far away from the rest of his *hās*, and therefore the tithing, at the tithing place, is delayed, and furthermore, even after tithing it is difficult to bring the tithe [tof these villages] together with the tithe of the rest of his *hās*. As compensation [for the two villages he has given up he has received] villages with a [total] registered yield of 9,550, in the aforementioned district in the subdistrict of Alacahisar, vacant from the deceased Hüseyin, and the village of درا سقو فجه,

with a registered yield of 2,500, in the subdistrict of دلبو صجه,
vacant from Vuk, non-Muslim, who was deserving of dismissal
for, as per his [Murad Bey's] own letter, he [Vuk] did not
attend the defense of Buda and the battle of Pest. To make up
[Murad Bey's] raise for the battle of Pest, vacant villages from
the *timar*s of some who are deceased and some who were
deserving of dismissal for not attending the defense of Buda, as
per his [Murad Bey's] own letter, with a [total] registered yield
of 32,337 *akçe*s, were brought together, and his total *hās* in the
amount of 283,222 *akçe*s, with a surplus of 942 *akçe*s which
cannot be separated, is submitted to that wish-granting abode
[i.e., the imperial palace] with the appointment certificate
[given by] this slave [i.e., the governor general] petitioning
that the *hās* be entered in the imperial register and the diploma
of office be granted in this amount. Written on the 28 Şaban
949.)

Figure 13. Initial appointment (f. 628a).

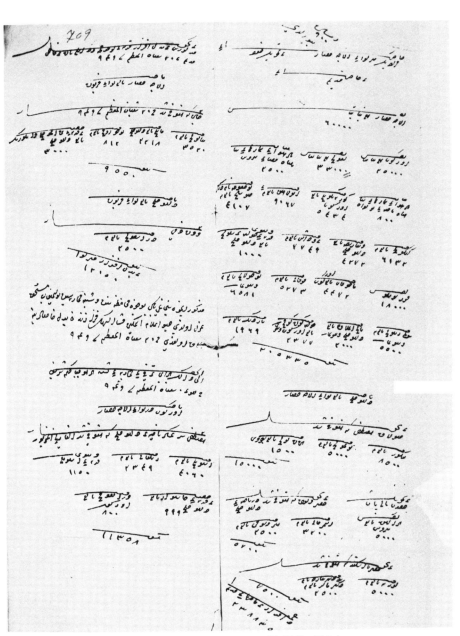

Figure 14. Raise in Revenues (ff. 708b–709a).

Figure 15. Raise in revenues (*cont.*) (ff. 709b–710b).

APPENDIX 4

Career Samples

1. İBRAHİM BEY

   MAD 563; Erzurum, p. 170: The *zeāmet* of İbrahim Bey, steward of the Erzurum province *timar* holders, former treasurer of the said province. (*Zeāmet-i İbrahim Bey, kethüdā-ı timarhā-ı vilāyet-i Erzurum, nāzır-ı sābık-ı vilāyet-i mezbūre.*) On 21 Rebi ül-ahır 972.
   Revenues (*hāsıl*) 65,460. *Berāt* (diploma of office) issued on the same date. (*Berāt şüd fi tārihih.*)
   (Next appointment on 22 Ramazan 975.)
   Length of office about $3\frac{1}{2}$ years. Out of office for 3 years.
   MAD 563; Erzurum, p. 169: The region of Tekman in the hand of İbrahim Bey, former steward of the Erzurum province *timar* holders. (*Nevāhi-i Tekmān der dest-i İbrahim Bey, kethüdā-ı sābık-ı timarhā-ı vilāyet-i Erzurum.*) On 25 Ramazan 978.
   Revenues 200,000. *Berāt* issued on the same date, with deficit. (*Berāt şüd bā noksan fi tārihih.*)
   New *berāt* issued, with surplus, in the year 980 (*def'a berāt şüd maa ziyāde fi sene 980*): 204,280.
   (Next appointment on 25 Muharrem 981.)
   Length of office 28 months. Reappointed immediately.
   MAD 563; Erzurum, p. 152: Oltu in the hand of İbrahim Bey, former governor of Tekman. (*Oltu der dest-i İbrahim Bey, mir-i sābık-ı Tekmān.*) On 28 Muharrem 981.
   Revenues 214,280. *Berāt* issued in the same year (*berāt şüd fi sene-i m [ezbūr]*).
   (Last entry; next appointment not entered.)
   KK 262; Şehrizul, p. 150: Karadağ an ülkā-ı Kara Kitmas (قره قيتماس).
   İbrahim Bey, governor of said district, was issued a *berāt* for a total of 218,200 *akçe*s, ·8,000 *akçe*s of his surplus *hās* having been ordered to

Hasan Paşa in Zilkade 981. (*Liva-ı mezbūr beyi İbrahim Bey icmāllu hāslarından sekiz bin akçesi Hasan Paşa'ya sene 981 Zilkade'sinde emr virilub cümle 218,200 akçe ile berāt itdi.*) On 1 Cemāzi ül-ahır 982.
(Next appointment on 28 Şaban 982.)
Length of office 9 months. Out of office for 22 months.

KK 262; Karaman, p. 48: Akşehir. The governor of Karadağ appointed; with same revenue, 218,201 *akçes*. (*218,201 akçe ile Karadağ beyi buyuruldu; bedeliyle.*) On 28 Cemāzi ül-ahır 984.
Berāt issued for 219,844 *akçes*; on 16 Safer 985.
(Next appointment on 11 Cemazi ül-ahır 985.)
Length of office 1 year. Out of office for 9 months.

KK 262; Rumeli, p. 266: Kırkkilisa. Given to İbrahim Bey, former governor of Akşehir with 219,844 *akçe* revenues, with same revenue. (*Sābıkā 219,844 akçe ile Akşehir beyi olan İbrahim Bey'e bedeliyle buyuruldu.*) On 7 Rebi ül-evvel 986.
Berāt issued for 239,844 akçes on 4 Rebi ül-evvel 988.
(Next appointment in 991.)
Length of office about 5 years.
Cannot be identified in *Sicill-i Osmāni*.

2. SİNAN BEY

MAD 653; Budin, p. 49: Peçuy in the possession of Sinan Bey, former governor of Kopan. (*Der tasarruf-u Sinan Bey, mir-i sābık-ı Kopan.*) On 12 Rebi ül-ahır 974. Revenues 275,000.
Berāt issued, with deficit, in 974.
(Next appointment on 22 Cemazi ül-evvel 975.)
Length of office 14 months. Reappointed immediately.

MAD 563; Budin, p. 55: Novigrad in the possession of Sinan Bey, former governor of Peçuy. On 22 Cemāzi ül-ula 975. Revenues 275,000.
Berāt issued, with deficit, 13 Rebi ül-evvel 976.
(Next appointment on 18 Şevval 977.)
Length of office 29 months. Reappointed immediately.

MAD 563; Budin, p. 54: Sigetvar in the hand of Sinan Bey, former governor of Novigrad. On 18 Şevval 977. Revenues 275,000.
Berāt issued, with surplus, for 330,000 in 979 [*sic*].
(Next appointment on 19 Şaban 978.)
Length of office 10 months. Reappointed immediately.

MAD 563; Tımışvar, p. 63: Arad maa Güle in the hand of Sinan Bey former governor of Sigetvar. On 19 Şaban 978. Revenues 275,000 [*sic*].
Berāt issued, with surplus, for 335,000.
(Next appointment on 23 Rebi ül-ahır 980.)
Length of office 20 months. Out of office for 5 months.

MAD 563; Budin, p. 50: Segedin in the hand of Sinan Bey, former governer of Güle. On 21 Ramazan 980. Revenues 335,000.
(Next appointment on 6 Rebi ül-evvel 981.)
Length of office 6 months.
Cannot be identified in *Sicill-i Osmāni.*

3. MUSTAFA BEY VELED-İ PERTEV PAŞA

MAD 563; Kaptan Paşa, p. 44: *Zeāmet* in the name of Mustafa Bey, son of Pertev Paşa, of the *müteferrika*s of the imperial palace; steward of the Cezair [Aegean islands] province timar holders. (*Zeāmet benām-ı Mustafa Bey veled-i hazret-i Pertev Paşa, an müteferrikayān-ı dergāh-ı āli; kethüdā-ı timarhā-ı vilāyet-i Cezāir [-i Bahr-i Sefid].*) On 15 Zilkāde 975. Revenues 93,000.
Berāt issued on the same date.
(Next appointment on 7 Rebi ül-ahır 978.)
Length of office 28 months. Reappointed immediately. District was without governor for two weeks.

MAD 563; Anadolu, p. 74: Alaiye in the hand of Mustafa Bey, son of Pertev Paşa, former steward of Cezair. On 20 Rebi ül-evvel 978. Revenues 350,000.
(Next appointment on 30 Rebi ül-ahır 978.)
Length of office 40 days. Reappointed immediately.

MAD 563; Anadolu, p. 75: Karesi in the hand of Mustafa Bey, son of Pertev Paşa, former governor of Alaiye. On 30 Rebi ül-ahır 978.
(Next appointment on 11 Ramazan 978.)
Length of office $4\frac{1}{2}$ months. Reappointed immediately.

MAD 563; Rum, p. 141: Amasya in the hand of Mustafa Bey, son of Pertev Paşa, former governor of Karesi. On 11 Ramazan 978. Revenues 350,000.
(Next appointment on 9 Safer 982.)
Length of office $3\frac{1}{2}$ years.
Cannot be identified in *Sicill-i Osmāni.* Father Pertev Mehmed Paşa (*SO,* 2:37–38) became vezir in 962, promoted to third vezir in 968 and second vezir in 972. Was the commander of Ottoman forces at the Lepanto defeat in 1571/979, upon which he was dismissed from office, and died in 982 still out of favor.

4. [ŞAH] MEHMED BEY VELED-İ FERHAD PAŞA

MAD 563; Erzurum, p. 149: Hınıs in the possession of Şah Mehmed Bey, former governor of Kars. On 29 Ramazan 973. Revenues 290,000.
Berāt issued in the year 974.
(Next appointment of 10 Cemazi ül-evvel 977.)
Length of office $3\frac{1}{2}$ years. Reappointed immediately.

MAD 563; Diyarbekir, p. 80: Kabur in the hand of Mehmed Bey,

former governor of Hınıs. Given with same revenue. On 10 Cemazi
ül-ula 977. Revenues 300,626. *Berāt* issued in 983.
(Next appointment on 18 Zilhicce 978.)
Length of office 1½ years. Reappointed immediately.
MAD 563; Bagdad, p. 107: Erbil in the hand of Mehmed Bey [Şah
before Mehmed crossed out], son of Ferhad Paşa, former governor
of Kabur. On 18 Zilhicce 978. Revenues 300,626.
(Next appointment on 28 Safer 979.)
Length of office 2½ months. Reappointed immediately.
MAD 563; Şam, p. 159: Safed in the hand of Mehmed Bey, son of
Ferhad Paşa, former governor of Erbil. On 28 Safer 979. Revenues
300,626. Correct (*sahh*),
(Next appointment on 9 Şevval 979.)
Length of office 8 months. Reappointed immediately.
MAD 563; Haleb, p. 167: Hama in the hand of Mehmed Bey, former
governor of Safed. On 7 Sevval 979. Revenues 300,626. Correct.
Berāt issued in 983 [*sic*].
(Next appointment on 20 Cemazi ül-ahir 980.)
Length of office 7 months.
Sicill-i Osmāni, 4:124. Mehmed Paşa, Solak Ferhad Paşa oğlu.
Served as district governor, holding Kastamonu, before being
promoted to governor general in 985, as *beylerbeyi* of Kars [a newly
created province; Kars was a district of Erzurum previously; Meh-
med Bey himself served there as *sancakbeyi* before 973]. Beylerbeyi of
Diyarbekir in 990. Killed in action during the Iranian campaigns,
in Şaban 992.

5. MEHMED BEY/PAŞA VELED-İ MUSTAFA PAŞA

MAD 563; Şam, p. 159: Safed in the possession of Mehmed Bey, son of
Mustafa Paşa the governor general of Şam, former governor of
Trablus. On 1 Zilkade 974. Revenues 394,575.
Berāt issued, with raise for accession [of the new sultan] and other
[purposes], on 15 Şevval 975 (*Berāt şüd maa terakki-i cülūs ve gayrihi*).
(Next appointment on 20 Safer 976.)
Length of office 15 months. Reappointed immediately.
MAD 563; Anadolu, p. 70: Ankara in the hand of Mehmed Bey,
former governor of Safed. On 20 Safer 976. Revenues 394,575.
(Next appointment on 18 Ramazan 976.)
Length of office 7 months. Reappointed immediately.
MAD 563; Karaman, p. 130: Niğde in the hand of Mehmed Bey,
former governor of Ankara. On 18 Ramazan 976. Revenues
394,575.
(Next appointment on 4 Rebi ül-ahir 979.)
Length of office 31 months. Reappointed immediately.
MAD 563; Dulkadriye, p. 134: Maraş [the seat of Dulkadriye prov-

ince; promoted to *beylerbeyi*] in the hand of Mehmed Paşa, son of
Mustafa Paşa, former governor of Niğde. On 28 Rebi ül-evvel 979.
Revenues 600,000.
Berāt issued, with surplus, in 980; 623,449.
(Next appointment on 27 Ramazan 980.)
MAD 563; Haleb, p. 168: Haleb in the hand of Mehmed Paşa, son of
Mustafa Paşa, former governor general of Maraş. On 27 Ramazan
980. Revenues 900,000.
His father, Mustafa Paşa, was governor general of Şam from 971
until 20 Safer 976, when he became a vezir of the imperial council;
note that father and son moved to new offices on the same date
(MAD 563, p. 161).
Sicill-i Osmāni, 4:121. Governor general of Musul [*sic*], Dulkadriye,
and Haleb. Died in Şevval 982, at the age of thirty. The people of
Haleb mourned his death for he had been a very good governor
general.

6. AHMED BEY VELED-İ İSKENDER PAŞA
MAD 563; Haleb, p. 165: Maarra in the possession of Ahmed Bey, son
of İskender Paşa, former governor of Çirmen. On 27 Cemazi ul-
evvel 978. Revenues 264,088. Raise 30,000 on the same date (*fi't-
tārih el-mezbūr*).
(Next appointment on 11 Cemazi ül-ahir 978.)
Length of office 3 years. Reappointed immediately.
MAD 563; Anadolu, p. 74: Hamid in the hand of Ahmed Bey, son of
İskender Paşa, former governor of Maarra. On 14 Cemazi ül-evvel
978. Revenues, with raises, 324,088.
Berāt issued, with deficit, in 979.
(Last entry; next appointment not entered.)
KK 262; Rum, p. 54: Divriği. Conferred on (*tevcīh olundu*) Ahmed Bey,
governor of Hamid, from 11 Cemazi ül-evvel 974, with same
revenue.
Took out *berāt* (*Berāt eyledi*), for 334,088 *akçe*s, on 29 Receb 985.
(Next appointment not entered.)
Length of office 15 months? Reappointed immediately?
KK 262; Karaman, p. 47: Niğde. Granted to (*buyuruldu*) Ahmed Bey,
former governor of Divriği. On 1 Şaban 985.
Took out *berāt*, for 344,088, on 9 Cemazi ül-ahir [98]6.
(Next appointment on 23 Muharrem 986.)
Length of office 5 months. Out of office for six months.
KK 262; Erzurum, p. 197: Trabzon. Granted to Ahmed Bey, governor
of Niğde with 344,088 *akçe*s, with same revenue. On 25 Receb 986.
Took out *berāt*, for 374,378 *akçe*s, on 29 Şaban 986.
(Next appointment on 11 Şevval 988.)
Length of office 27 months. Reappointed immediately (next entry

reads: Ahmed Bey, the governor of Trabzon, being granted another district/*Trabzon beyi Ahmed Bey'e gayri sancak virilüb* ...). *Sicill-i Osmāni*, 1 : 202. Ahmed Paşa, son of Çerkes İskender Paşa. Served as district governor. Appointed *beylerbeyi* of Lahsa. Took part in the Iranian campaigns. Appointed *beylerbeyi* of Rakka. Died in 987 [*sic*]. *Selāniki*, p. 238. News reached İstanbul in late Rebi ül-evvel 996 that İskender Paşazāde, the governor general of Rakka died.

Notes

Method and Sources

1. David Ayalon, *L'Esclavage du Mamelouk*, and *Gunpowder and Firearms in the Mamluk Kingdom*. On Mamluks under Ottoman rule, see Ayalon, "Studies in al-Jabarti," *JESHO* (1960), 3:148–74, 275–325; P. M. Holt, *Egypt and the Fertile Crescent*; Holt, "The Pattern of Egyptian Political History from 1517 to 1798."

2. Mustafa Akdağ, *Celâli İsyanları* (Celali Revolts); Akdağ, "Genel Çizgileriyle XVII. Yüzyıl Türkiye Tarihi" (Outlines of Seventeenth-Century Turkish History); Halil İnalcık, "Adaletnameler" (Fermans of Justice); İnalcık, *The Ottoman Empire: The Classical Age, 1300–1600*. Note that İnalcık's title proclaims the date 1600 as the main turning point in Ottoman history; Ömer L. Barkan, "The Price Revolution of the Sixteenth Century: A Turning Point in the Economic History of the Near East."

3. Yaşar Yücel, ed., *Kitāb-ı Müstetāb*; Ali Kemāli Aksüt, ed., *Koçi Bey Risalesi*; Katib Çelebi, *Düstūr el-Amel li-islāh el-Halel*.

4. İ. Metin Kunt, "The Köprülü Years: 1656–1661."

5. On an earlier phase of this research see İ. Metin Kunt, "Ethnic-Regional (*Cins*) Solidarity in the Seventeenth-Century Ottoman Establishment."

6. For an excellent discussion on the method and its place in current historiography see Lawrence Stone, "Prosopography." Stone's *The Crisis of The Aristocracy: 1558–1641* (Oxford, 1965) is a masterful example of the uses of the method.

7. N. Itzkowitz, "Eighteenth Century Ottoman Realities," *Studia Islamica* (1962), 16:73–94.

8. N. Itzkowitz and Joel Shinder, "The Office of Şeyh ül-Islām and the Tanzimat—A Prosopographic Enquiry."

9. Faroqhi, "Social Mobility and the Ottoman 'Ulema in the Late Sixteenth Century"; Ali Uğur, "The Ottoman Ulema in the Mid-17th Century: An Analysis of the *Vakā'i'ül-Fuzalā* of Mehmed Şeyhi Efendi."

10. Abou-el-Haj, "The Ottoman Vezir and Paşa Households, 1683–1703: A Preliminary Report." I maintain that by the late seventeenth century that the author studies, the crucial changes had already taken place; also his categorization of the military fails to make the basic distinction between provincial and central groups.

11. For the development of history in Islamic civilization see H. A. R. Gibb, "Tarikh"; Franz Rosenthal, *A History of Muslim Historiography*.

12. For an interesting recent study see Richard W. Bulliet, "A Quantitative Approach to Medieval Muslim Biographical Dictionaries."

13. İ. H. Uzunçarşılı, *Osmanlı Tarihi* (Ottoman History); İ. H. Danişmend, *İzahlı Osmanlı Tarihi Kronolojisi* (Annotated Chronology of Ottoman History).
14. Marija Dukanoviç, ed., *Rimovana Autobiografija Varvari Ali-Paşe.*
15. Evliya Çelebi, *Seyahatname* (Travels).
16. Katib Çelebi, *The Balance of Truth.*

1. The Emergence of the Ottoman State

1. The classic works on the emergence of the Ottoman state are Paul Wittek, *The Rise of the Ottoman Empire* and M. Fuad Köprülü, *Les Origines de l'Empire Ottoman.*
2. A new analysis of early Ottoman society is in Rudi Paul Lindner, "Ottoman Government and Nomad Society," especially ch. 2: "Ottoman Success and Ottoman Settlements," pp. 15–61.
3. For the early development of the Ottoman state, see, in addition to works cited above, Paul Wittek, "De la défaite d'Ankara à la prise de Constantinople"; Halil İnalcık, "Ottoman Methods of Conquest." For a recent article outlining pitfalls of generalizations about sources and character of early Ottoman institutions see Joel Shinder, "Early Ottoman Administration in the Wilderness: Some Limits on Comparison."
4. Halil İnalcık, "Balaban," *EI* (2).
5. V. L. Ménage, "Beylerbey," and H. İnalcık, "Eyalet," both in *EI* (2). The *beylerbeyi* continued to proliferate as the state grew in territory: a fourth one was created after the conquest of Karaman lands in central Anatolia in the 1460s; others appeared in the first decades of the sixteenth century in eastern Anatolia (Diyarbekir) and in Arab lands (at first a single one, called Arab province, which was soon divided into the provinces of Egypt and Damascus). By the middle of the century there were about twenty provinces and close to forty in the early 1600s. In the fifteenth century the *kadıasker*, too, was territorialized, one for European territories and one for the east, but unlike the *beylerbeyi*, there was no further proliferation and both *kadıasker*s resided in the capital.
6. This shift in the nature of the vezirate lends itself to an alternate interpretation. İnalcık, for example, sees the change primarily as a shift away from native Muslims in favor of slaves and only secondarily, because native Muslims tended to be learned bureaucrats and slaves mainly military men, as a change in the nature of the office: *The Ottoman Empire: The Classical Age, 1300–1600*, p. 77; for İnalcık's comments on the—later—vezir as military commander, see p. 95.
7. For full annotation on palace organization and the slave system, see chapter 3.

2. Provincial Administration

1. BA, MAD 17893, a register of *dirlik* grants (*rūznamçe*) in the Anatolian provinces for the years 892–94/1486–88: p. 200, a *timar* of 21,000 *akçes*; p. 305, a *timar* of 14,746 *akçes* granted *ber vech-i zeāmet/*as a *zeāmet*. BA, KK 697, *dirlik* register (*icmāl defter*) for Hersek (Herzegovina) district, originally prepared in 904/1498: f. 15b, a *zeāmet* which was increased to 20,000 *akçes* in 908. *Akçe* was the small silver coin of the Ottomans, the main monetary unit

in the classical period. One gold piece was worth about 50 *akçe*s around 1500. See H. Bowen, "Akçe," *EI* (2).

2. BA, MAD 34, *rūznamçe* for the Balkan provinces for the years 948–49/1541–42: f. 320b, *timar* of 130,000 *akçe*s granted to a retired *beylerbeyi.* Such duplication of terms occurs frequently in Ottoman usage. Perhaps the most vexing term is *sipāhi*, cavalry or cavalryman: it is used to mean *timar*-holding provincial cavalry as well as to refer to the household (*kapıkulu*) cavalry; to further complicate the situation, one of the six regiments of the household cavalry is itself called *sipāhi.*

3. The use of terms of horsemanship in military-administrative contexts is of old standing. Another Ottoman example is *arpalık*, literally "for barley," i.e., to feed horses; the term was used to refer to large *dirlik*s granted to officials of high rank who were retired or were temporarily out of office (i.e., without appointment to a particular post). So also *ulūfe*, literally "fodder, forage," was the term for the quarterly payments to central army (*kapıkulu*) troops.

4. Only in the mid-sixteenth century do we find *timar*s made up of some urban revenues (an example is in MAD 34, f. 137a), but by then the term was devoid of functional significance, referring only to *dirlik*s below 20,000 *akçe*s.

5. H. İnalcık, in his standard discussion of provincial administration, *The Ottoman Empire: The Classical Age, 1300–1600* pp. 104–18, has pointed this out (p. 108). For the dirlik system see also Ö. L. Barkan, "Timar," *IA.*

6. İnalcık also refers to the *sancak* as the principal administrative unit. *The Ottoman Empire*, pp. 72 and 117.

7. At least one modern scholar has treated the terms *sancakbeyi* and *atlu sancakbeyi* as separate offices, Mustafa Akdağ, *Türkiye'nin İktisadi ve İçtimai Tarihi* (The Economic and Social History of Turkey), (Istanbul, 1974), 1:407, 415; (Ankara, 1971), 2:29. But their interchangeable use in district regulations (*sancak kānūnnāme*s) proves beyond doubt that they designated the same person. See the texts published by Ömer Lütfi Barkan, *XV ve XVIıncı Asırlarda Osmanlı İmparatorluğunda Zirāi Ekonominin Hukuki ve Māli Esasları, I: Kanunlar* (The Legal and Fiscal Bases of Agricultural Economy in the Ottoman Empire in the 15th and 16th Centuries, I: Regulations), p. 5, Hüdavendigār, article 29; p. 27, Kütahya, art. 21; p. 70, Erzurum, art. 44; p. 180, Musul, art. 28; p. 268, Nigbolu, art. 8; p. 396, Bosna, art. 4.

8. Examples can be found in Aşıkpaşazāde's fifteenth-century chronicle: *Aşıkpaşazāde Tarihi*, Ali Bey, ed., pp. 172 and 174: "*Anadolu askerinden bir nice sancak ...*" (many district commands from among Anatolian troops).

9. The standard discussion of these terms and processes is in H. İnalcık, "Ottoman Methods of Conquest."

10. An example is to be found in the preamble of the *kānūnnāme* of Erzurum, dated 1540: Barkan, *Kanunlar*, p. 63.

11. Barkan, *Kanunlar*, Erzurum: p. 181, dated 1516 and p. 62, dated 1540; Budin-Estergon-Hatvan-Novigrad: p. 303, dated 1545. While there were separate *kānūnnāme*s for certain other Hungarian *sancak*s they varied little in content.

12. For examples of different appointees holding the same post with varying levels of *hās*, see the sample pages from the *ümerā* appointment registers provided in appendix 2.

13. *Sūret-i Defter-i Sancak-ı Arvānid* (Copy of the Register of the District of Albania), Halil İnalcık, ed., p. 1: "*Hāshā-ı Sancakbeyi der tasarruf-u Ali Beg*" (The *hās* of the *sancakbeyi* in the possession of Ali Beg). For similar expressions see Tayyib Gökbilgin, "XVI. Asır Başlarında Kayseri ve Livası," (Kayseri and its District in the Early 16th Century), especially pp. 97–98 and 100–5.

14. See appendix 2 for this register.

15. This section is based on a paper presented at the First International Congress on the Economic and Social History of Turkey (Ankara, 1977), where I analyzed the *hās* entries for about 40 *sancakbeyi* appointments to various districts in the Balkan and Anatolian areas of the empire in the period 1480–1540, and computed for each *hās* the percentage of revenues from towns, *sancak*-wide revenues (*niyābet*, see below), villages with revenues above 20,000 *akçes*, those yielding above 10,000 akçes, revenues from smaller villages, and revenues from nomads. The findings confirm impressions of earlier researchers: Tayyib Gökbilgin, *XV.–XVI. Asırlarda Edirne ve Paşa Livası* (Edirne and the Paşa District in the 16th–17th Centuries), p. 83, and H. İnalcık, *Suret-i Defter-i . . .*, p. xxvii.

16. See, for example, appendix 3 for a *sancakbeyi* requesting a change in villages included in his *hās* on this basis.

17. Some registers record urban revenues as a lump sum, under the rubric *nefs-i şehr* or *nefs-i x*. In the following examples the composition of urban revenues is detailed and in some cases the amount of revenue from each source is also specified: Vılçitrin, dated 892/1498, BA TD, 22; Semendire, 932/1526, BA TD, 135; Alaiye, 927/1521, BA TD, 107; Karaman, 929/1523, BA TD, 119.

18. For example, Alaiye, 927/1521, BA TD, 107; Hamid, 927/1521, BA TD, 107; Beyşehri, 929/1523, BA TD, 119. İnalcık notes that as a rule the *cizye* was collected directly by the sultan: "*Djizya*—The Ottoman Empire," *EI* (2).

19. Various fines and taxes included under the heading *ādet-i emīrāne* in the registers of Karaman province (e.g., BA TD, 11; TD, 118, both from the 15208s) are the same as those included under *niyābet* elsewhere.

20. For a general discussion see H. İnalcık, "Adaletnāmeler" (Fermans of Justice), 7:(3–4) 80–82.

21. Barkan, *Kanunlar*, Regulations for Niğbolu district, p. 268, article 10; Silistre, p. 274, article 12.

22. Barkan, *Kanunlar*, Kayseri, p. 57, article 4. It seems that in the sixteenth century the trend was to abolish the *sancakbeyi*'s share in the yoke tax: Hamid, pp. 32–33, article 1, and Ankara, p. 44.

23. It is difficult to ascertain the correspondance between the two different subdivisions of a district, i.e., between *nāhiye*s, the chief towns of which were under command of a *zeāmet* holder (*zaīm, subaşı*) or of an officer of the governor's retinue if the town was included in his *hās*, and the *kaza*s. In some districts a *nāhiye* and a *kazā* referred to the same area, but it seems that more often they did not and a *kazā* included more than one *nāhiye*s.

24. Cf. indexes of published imperial *kānūnnāme*s (codes of regulations): Robert Anhegger and H. İnalcık eds., *Kānūnnāme-i Sultāni ber mūceb-i Örf-i Osmānī*; Nicoara Beldiceanu, ed., *Les Actes des Premiers Sultans, I: Actes de Mehmed II et de Bayezid II du MS. Fonds Turc Ancien 39*, and *Les Actes des Premiers Sultans, II: Règlements Miniers, 1390–1512.*

25. Many documents in the Ottoman archives contain such special orders. For some published examples see: Tayyib Gökbilgin, "Venedik Devlet Arşivindeki Vesikalar Külliyatında Kanuni Sultan Süleyman Devri Belgeleri" (Documents from the Period of Suleyman I in the Holdings of the Venetian State Archives); and "Venedik Devlet Arşivindeki Türkçe Belgeler Koleksiyonu ve Bizimle İlgili Diğer Belgeler" (The Turkish Documents Collection in the Venetian State Archives and Other Documents Concerning Us [i.e., the Ottoman Empire]), Documents 52, 56, 62, 101, 163.

26. Gökbilgin, documents 55, 57, 59–60, 63, 100, 105, 111, 140–41, 143, 145, 148, 156–62.

27. Gökbilgin, documents 37–38, 46, 103, 124–25, 200.

28. İnalcık, *The Ottoman Empire*, p. 113.

29. At least during the fifteenth century the *icmāl* registers, recording all *dirlik*s in a given district, carefully noted the number of men and the type of equipment each *dirlik* holder was required to bring on campaigns. See, for example, İnalcık, *Sūret-i Defter-i* . . . , headings of *dirlik* entries.

30. Mentioned in district regulations: Barkan, *Kanunlar*, Erzurum, p. 68, article 35; Niğbolu, p. 271, article 32. The wedding dues point to the hierarchical arrangement: *sancakbeyi* daughters paid them to the *beylerbeyi*, *beylerbeyi* daughters paid them to the sultan. Wedding dues from the subjects were shared by the *sancakbeyi* and the *timar* holders (Barkan, "Timar," *İA*, p. 309). In some *sancak*s the *timar* holder kept the *reāyā* wedding dues (*Kanunlar*, Gelibolu, p. 236, article 7; İmroz, p. 239, article 10).

31. *Kanunlar*, Niğbolu, pp. 267–68, article 5; Hatvan, p. 371, article 13.

32. *Kanunlar*, Niğbolu, p. 267, article 4.

33. As an example of how serious the differences could be, even for neighboring *sancak*s, see Bruce McGowan's important study: "Food Supply and Taxation on the Middle Danube (1568–1579)." Variations *within* a district also obtained. See *Kanunlar*, Aydın, p. 16; Bolu, p. 29.

34. Uriel Heyd, *Studies in Old Ottoman Criminal Law*, V. L. Ménage, ed., p. 90, article 118.

35. *Kanunlar*, Niğbolu, pp. 268 and 267, and Bosna, p. 395.

36. For a fifteenth-century diploma of office (*berāt*) for a *beylerbeyi* see Necati Lugal and Adnan Erzi, eds., *Fatih Devrine Ait Münşeat Mecmuası* (A Document Handbook-Anthology from the Period of the Conqueror), document 48, pp. 73–74, dated 1468.

37. But copies of *sancak* surveys have also come to light in *sancak* seats: Amnon Cohen and Bernard Lewis, *Population and Revenue in the Towns of Palestine in the Sixteenth Century*, p. 4.

38. Such grants were called *tezkeresiz*, without certificate. The limits of *timars* the *beylerbeyi* could grant directly were different for Anatolia and for the Balkans. İnalcık, *The Ottoman Empire*, p. 114.

3. The *Ümerā* Status

1. Niccolò Machiavelli, *The Prince* (New York: New American Library, 1959), section 4, pp. 43–45.

2. C. T. Forster and F. H. Blackburne Daniell, trans., *The Life and Letters of Ogier Ghiselin de Busbecq* (London, 1881), 1 : 154–55 and *passim*.

3. For the *mamluk* slave institution in Islamic history, see the works of David Ayalon, the most prominent researcher in this field: *L'Esclavage du Mamelouk*; Ayalon, *Gunpowder and Firearms in the Mamluk Kingdom*, and more recently, "Aspects of the Mamluk Phenomenon." Also see "Ghulam," *EI* (2); Paul G. Forand, "The Relation of the Slave and the Client to the Master or Patron."

4. For various aspects of the slave system in the Ottoman empire see: H. İnalcık, "Ghulam, Part IV, Ottoman Empire," *EI* (2); H. İnalcık, *The Ottoman Empire: The Classical Age, 1300–1600*; H. A. R. Gibb and Harold Bowen, *Islamic Society and the West*, İ. H. Uzunçarşılı, *Kapıkulu Ocakları* (Household Troops); A. H. Lybyer, *The Government of the Ottoman Empire at the Times of Suleiman the Magnificent*; Barnette Miller, *The Palace School of*

Mohammad the Conqueror; V. L. Ménage, "Devshirme," *EI* (2); Basilike D. Papoulia, *Ursprung und Wesen der Knabenlese im Osmanischen Reich*; V. L. Ménage, "Some Notes on the Devshirme"; P. Wittek, *"Devshirme* and *Shari'a"*; Norman Itzkowitz, "Eighteenth Century Ottoman Realities"; Metin Kunt, "Kulların Kulları" (Slaves of Slaves).

5. See Ayalon, *L'Esclavage du Mamelouk, passim,* and Metin Kunt, "Ethnic-Regional (*Cins*) Solidarity in the Seventeenth-Century Ottoman Establishment."

6. İnalcık, *The Ottoman Empire,* p. 81.

7. Lütfi Paşa, *Asāfnāme,* p. 24: "Ve reayadan olub ata ve dededen sipahizade olmayanı sipahi etmede dayanmak gerek; ol kapu açılınca herkes raiyetlikten kaçup sipahi olmak lazım gelür." But elsewhere Lütfi Paşa recognizes that *reaya* may deserve *timar* grants (p. 43).

8. This edict, along with others on *timar* regulations in a manuscript in the Bibliothèque Nationale, has been published in paraphrase by M. Tayyib Gökbilgin, "Kanuni Sultan Süleyman'ın Timar ve Zeāmet Tevcihi ile Ilgili Fermanları" (Fermans of Süleyman I on Timar and Zeāmet Grants), Document No. 1. The quotation is from a copy of the *ferman* in a collection of *kanunname* (regulations) in Atıf Efendi Library (Istanbul) MS. 1734, f. 2a.

9. The following registers contain many examples of such lists: BA, KK 320 (dated 990/1582) and KK 342 (dated 1002–03/1593–95).

10. Gökbilgin, Document 1.

11. Gökbilgin, "Müteferrika," *İA*.

12. BA, MAD 559, pp. 5–7. The three groups of *müteferrika* are called "Cemaat-i Müteferrika ki be-hizmet-i hassa tayin bude end," "Cemaat-i evlād ve ihvān-ı vüzerā ve gayrihi der müteferrika," "Cemaat-i müteferrika-i saire." A similar list was published by Ö. L. Barkan, "H.933–934 (M.1527–28) Mali Yılına ait bir Bütçe Örneği," *İFM* (1953–54), 15:250–329, appendix 5, pp. 316–21. In it the second group is separated into two, *"Cemaat-i evlad-ı ümera ve ihvan-ı vüzera"* and *"Cemaat-i evlad-ı ümera-ı* (illegible) *ve evlad-ı miran-ı elviye,"* with six and thirty-two persons respectively. Barkan's register (TSA, D.7843) is undated, but from a comparison of the pay to some persons who appear on both lists, it seems to be slightly earlier than MAD 559, despite Barkan's guess that it dates from the mid to late 940s (1530s).

13. Lütfi Paşa *Asāfnāme,* p. 21, "Ve ulûfe müteferrikalığı haricden olanlara virilmemek gerekdir, illa harem-i hāsdan çıka yahud beylerbeyi ve defterdār oğulları ola."

14. In Barkan's list they appear in Group 3, *Cemaat-i Yeniçeriyān:* #8, "Ahmed Bey, ağa-i ebnā-i sipāhiyan, Ayas Paşa hazretlerinin kardeşidir"; and #17 *Ahmed Bey, ser atmacacıyān, Kızıl Ahmedoğlu* (i.e., of the İsfendiyar family) *Mahmud Ağa ki çakırcıbaşı olmuştur anın oğludur."*

15. One such case I have come across is *"Bāli Bey, Kethüdā-ı Hazret-i İbrahim Paşa,"* who appears under *"Cemaat-i Müteferrika-ı saire"* in both TSA, D.7843, and MAD 559 (identified there as *"Kethüdā-ı Hazret-i Serasker Sultan"*). It is common knowledge to Ottoman scholars that İbrahim Paşa, the master of Bāli Bey, himself had an extremely exceptional career as a result of his close relationship with Sultan Süleyman.

16. Gökbilgin, Document 6.

17. BA, KK 697.

18. BA, MAD 34.

19. *Tārih-i Peçuyi,* 1:10,115.

20. V. L. Ménage, "Some Notes on the *Devşirme.*" This is the most thorough discussion on the subject to date.

21. Ménage, "Some Notes," p. 66. The quotation was taken from the officer's report submitted upon his return; it was published by Şerafettin Turan in *Belleten* (1962), 26:(103) 539–55.

22. These lists are discussed in appendix 1: one of them, TSA D.5246, which is the basis for table 3.3, is given there in text, translation, and facsimile.

23. This information totally invalidates the view that from the time of Mehmed II (second half of the fifteenth century) on the slaves (*gulām*) took over all important administrative positions. For a recent and extreme statement of this view see Yaşar Yücel, "Osmanlı İmparatorluğunda Desantralizasyona Dair Genel Gözlemler" (General Observations on Decentralization in the Ottoman Empire), especially pp. 660–62.

24. İnalcık, *The Ottoman Empire*, p. 87.

25. L. Fekete, *Die Siyaqāt-schrift in der Türkischen Finanzverwaltung*, Document 7: Ottoman original and German translation, 1:170–75; facsimile, vol. 2, plate 9; M. Kunt, "Kulların Kulları."
I am preparing two more lists, TPA D.10087 and TPA D.9189, for publication; these lists have been introduced in a research note in the *Turkish Studies Association Bulletin*, 1979.

26. Gelibolulu Mustafa Āli, *Mevāidü'n-Nefāis fi Kavāidi'l-Mecālis*, pp. 29–30.

27. TSA D.10087.

28. Kunt, "Kulların Kulları," p. 29.

29. Kunt, "Kulların Kulları," p. 30.

30. İnalcık, *The Ottoman Empire*, pp. 83–4.

31. *Tārih-i Naīmā*, 5:280.

32. M. Kunt, "Ethnic-Regional (*Cins*) Solidarity in Seventeenth-Century Ottoman Empire."

33. İnalcık, *The Ottoman Empire*, p. 87.

34. Ö. L. Barkan, "Edirne Askeri Kassamına Ait Tereke Defterleri (1545-1659)" (Estate Registers of the Edirne *Askeri* Inheritance Authority); see pp. 147–51, items 84–115.

35. Barkan, "Kassam," pp. 387–91.

36. The date of death in the case of Ahmed Bey/Paşa, son of İskender Paşa (appendix 4, sample 6) is another example of the inaccuracy of *Sicill-i Osmāni*.

37. BA, KK. 717.

38. BA, KK. 1865.

39. BA, MAD. 17893, p. 132.

40. One reason, among several others, why Irene Beldiceanu-Steinherr doubts the authenticity of a *sancakbeyi* appointment certificate purported to be from the late fourteenth century is that the governor was given one million *akçe*s as *hās* which Beldiceanu-Steinherr thinks is unacceptably high. This *sancak* appointment, too, was in the frontier region. I. Beldiceanu-Steinherr, *Recherches sur les actes des regnes des sultans Osman, Orkhan et Murad I*, document no. 44. Our example, though one century later, at least indicates it was possible, if highly improbably, for a *sancakbeyi* to be allowed such a high income. This point, therefore, cannot be used to brand the fourteenth-century document as spurious. The document is given in a sixteenth-century collection: Feridun Ahmed Bey, *Münşeāt üs-Selātīn*, 1:87–9.

41. Agricultural land was similarly graded for purposes of the *çift* (yoke) tax, the basic tax on peasants: a smaller plot of good land was considered one *çift* than that of poorer, less productive land.

42. Uriel Heyd, *Studies in Old Ottoman Criminal Law*, translation on p. 95, text on p. 56.

43. İnalcık, *The Ottoman Empire*, p. 162.

44. Haim Gerber, "Seventeenth-Century Anatolian City of Bursa," Ph.D. diss., Hebrew University, 1976. English translation forthcoming.

45. Barkan, "Kassam." Estate listed on pp. 116–19, Barkan's comments on p. 114.

46. The list being incomplete the sum is not entered. Barkan computed the total variously, 95,250.50 *akçe*s on p. 119 and 100,721 *akçe*s on p. 460.

47. Barkan, "Kassam." Estate listed on pp. 147–51, Barkan's comments on pp. 132–33.

48. İalcık, "Capital Accumulation in the Ottoman Empire."

49. For Barkan's discussion of categories see pp. 455–59.

50. Ö. L. Barkan and Ekrem Ayverdi, *İstanbul Vakıfları Tahrir Defteri*, pp. xxivff.

4. The Structure of the Military-Administrative Career

1. *Koçi Bey Risalesi*, pp. 58 and 59.

5. Transformation of Provincial Administration

1. Readers familiar with Ottoman historiography will recognize that I tend to discount the more prevalent explanation of the slowing down of Ottoman Conquest, namely that Buda was the farthest the Ottoman central army could travel from Istanbul within one campaign season and hope to be back before the winter set in. This argument seems a partial one, for on the eastern front the same army was able to travel longer distances and stay in the field, if need be, over the winter. Also, developing regional armies would have been a solution if the distance were the only problem. I argue below that in the seventeenth century the governor general became a much more powerful figure in Ottoman administration than before; this development may have been due, among other reasons, to the necessity of establishing regional armies capable of undertaking operations on their own.

2. On this literature see Bernard Lewis, "Ottoman Observers of Ottoman Decline."

3. *Usūl el-Hikem fi Nizām ül-Ālem*.

4. C. T. Forster and F. H. Blackburne Daniell, trans., *The Life and Letters of Ogier Ghiselin de Busbecq*. (London, 1881), 1:242–43.

5. Ottoman use of firearms and artillery is well-known and requires no further comment. A recent article may be noted in this context for the description of *yeniçeri*s arranged in battle in two groups, one firing while the other was loading: Aryeh Shmuelevitz, "Capsali as a Source for Ottoman History, 1450–1523," especially p. 343. David Ayalon's classic work, *Gunpowder and Firearms in the Mamluk Kingdom*, is to date the most detailed study of the topic in the near east. Ayalon concludes that the Mamluks lost out to the Ottomans as the predominant power in the eastern Mediterranean because, while the *yeniçeri*s readily took to firearms, Mamluk cavalry rejected them. Busbecq's comment shows that the Ottoman *sipāhi*, on the other hand, was no different than the Mamluk cavalry.

6. Halil İnalcık, *The Ottoman Empire: The Classical Age, 1300–1600*, p. 83.

7. The process is best described in a forthcoming article in *Archivum Ottomanicum* by H. İnalcık on military and fiscal reorganization.

8. H. İnalcık, "The Heyday and Decline of the Ottoman Empire."

9. M. A. Cook, *Population Pressure in Rural Anatolia, 1450–1600*.

10. Mustafa Akdağ, *Celâli İsyanları* (Celâli Revolts).

11. Halil İnalcık, "Sekbanlar" (Mercenaries).

12. Barkan, "The Price Revolution of the Sixteenth Century: A Turning Point in the

Economic History of the Near East." This article is the somewhat streamlined and generalized version of an earlier work of the author, "XVI. Yüzyılın İkinci Yarısında Türkiye'de Fiat Hareketleri" (Price Movements in Turkey in the Second Half of the Sixteenth Century).

13. Haim Gerber, too, cautions against exaggerating the impact of the inflation in a forthcoming article: "The Monetary System of the Ottoman Empire."

14. Bruce McGowan, "Food Supply and Taxation on the Middle Danube (1568–1579)."

15. Robert Mantran, *Istanbul dans la seconde moitié du 17e siècle.*

16. Peçuylu İbrahim, *Tārih-i Peçüyi* (Istanbul, 1281–83), 1:8ff.

17. Cengiz Orhonlu, *Telhisler* (Reports of Grand Vezirs), p. 18, report no. 18: *Hākim namında olan kullarınızda kuvvet ve kudret ve māl ü mināl olmamağla gerek vüzera, gerekse beylerbeyiler ve beyler evvelki gibi yarar ve müstevfā adamlar saklamağa kimesnede istitā' at kalmamışdır, ānın içün düşmen dahi galebe eder olmuşdur. Bir kulunuza hidmet buyurulsa izhār-ı fakr edüp saadetli padişahımdan yükler ile akçe ister oldular. Ve bi'l-cümle bu makūle kullarunuzda māl ve kuvvet ve kudret olıcak asla yabana gitmeyüp ol malun menfaati cānib-i din ü devlete rāci olmak mukarrerdir.*

18. *Tārih-i Peçuyi,* 1:10, 115. The following *timar*-grant registers also contain many notations of *timars* given to *ümerā* retinues: BA, KK 320 (dated 990/1582) and KK 342 (dated 1002–3/1593–95).

19. Some examples: Mustafa Selānikī, *Selānikī Tārihi,* pp. 12, 14, 170, 191, 281, 319–20; Mustafa Naīmā, *Tārih-i Naīmā,* 1:79, 101, 200, 277, 324–25.

20. BA, MAD 17893, p. 208: "*Vilāyet-i Karaman, Karye-i Reis, tābi-i Akşehir. Zikr olan karye sahibinden hācet olup bilā sebep alınıp Uçarı Bey bu defa Şamlu muharebesinde yoldaşlık itdiği sebepten çiftlik tarikiyle emr olunup berāt-ı humāyūn için tezkere virildi. 5 Muharrem 894.*"

21. BA, TD 118.

22. BA, MAD 34, ff. 136a, 188b, 190b, 451b, 691a. The last two citations refer to the same *bey*'s appointment to two different *sancaks*. The characteristic notation is: "*müşārileyh her kande sancak tasarruf ider ise zikr olan karye bile mahsub oluna deyu ferman olunmağın deftere kayd olundu.*" (f. 451b). Also see BA, TD 269: Köstendil register dated 957/1549, the *sancakbeyi hās.*

23. BA, MAD 34, ff. 334b–335a, 476b, 635b. Also see BA, TD 269, Köstendil register, the *beylerbeyi hās.*

24. BA, MAD 34, f. 476b.

25. MAD 563: p. 48, Pojega, Mehmed Bey; p. 215, Bosna, Hasan Paşa; p. 37, Rumeli *timar defterdarı,* Mustafa Çelebi; p. 49, Peçuy, Ferhad Bey; p. 50, Segedin, Ali Bey; p. 51, Sirem, Mehmed Bey; p. 52, Şimontorna, İskender Bey; p. 53, Filek, Ali Bey; p. 66, Tımışvar *timar defterdarı,* Muharrem Çelebi; p. 70, Karahisar-i Sāhib, Mehmed Bey; p. 78, Diyarbekir, Hüseyin Paşa; p. 148, Pasin, Sinan Bey; KK 262: p. 8, Klis, Sinan Bey; p. 169, Lahsa, Mehmed Paşa; p. 202, Mamirvan, second entry (unnamed); p. 249, Şemāhi, Mustafa Paşa.

26. One exception is a *zaīm* who kept his *zeāmet* of 32,504 *akçes* as permanently granted revenues to be counted towards his *hās* when he was first promoted to *sancakbeyi* rank with a 200,000 *akçe hās*: KK 262, p. 202, Mamirvan, second entry. Even here the *zeāmet* accounted for only 16 percent of the *hās.*

27. See Halil İnalcık, "Çiftlik," *EI*(2), where examples of mid-fifteenth-century *ber vech-i çiftlik* grants as well as later ones are cited and labeled "personal estates."

28. Already in the 1570s Kastamonu was given twice as *arpalık* to beylerbeyis: MAD 563, p. 72: to Muzaffer Paşa, formerly governor of Bağdad, and to Mustafa Bey, formerly governor of Zulkadriye (Maraş).

29. Nedim Filipoviç, "Bosna-Hersek'te Timar Sisteminin İnkişafinda Bazi Hususiyetler" (Some Features in the Development of the *Timar* System in Bosnia-Herzegovina).

30. For an example see appendix 2, sample pages from Cev. Dah. 6095 and KK 266: Cafer Bey was appointed *sancakbeyi* of Prizrin "by intercession of the commander of the imperial guards" (*bā ricā-ı ser bostanciyān-i hassa*).

31. Cev. Dah. 6095: p. 37, Kastamonu, Ahmed Bey; p. 38, Karesi, Mustafa Bey; p. 47, Safed-Sayda-Beyrut, Abdurrahman Bey. The first two examples are reappointments, the last a promotion.

32. For some earlier instances of the phenomenon see Orhonlu, *Telhisler*, pp. 98, 108. The importance of households in advancement was also noted by Mustafa Akdağ, "Genel Çizgileriyle XVII. Yüzyıl Türkiye Tarihi" (Outlines of Seventeenth-Century Turkish History).

33. Ömer Lütfi Barkan, "Edirne Askeri Kassamına Ait Tereke Defterleri (1545–1659)" (Estate Registers of the Edirne *Askeri* Inheritance Authority), pp. 190–92, 236–38.

34. See under provinces named in KK 266 and Cev. Dah. 6095.

35. Halil İnalcık, "Adaletnameler" (Fermans of Justice), especially pp. 69–72.

36. M. A. Cook, *Population Pressure in Rural Anatolia*, p. 40.

37. *Tārih-i Naimā*, 3 : 134–42.

38. BA, MAD 6786. Commenting on Diyarbekir in 1655 Evliya Çelebi writes that the governor's proceeds amount to 100,000 *kuruş* (4 : 29).

39. Stanford J. Shaw, *The Financial and Administrative Organization and Development of Ottoman Egypt*, pp. 187–88, 291, 318–28.

40. Barkan, "The Price Revolution," p. 17, as measured in gold pieces.

41. İ. Metin Kunt, "Derviş Mehmed Paşa, Vezir and Entrepreneur: A Study in Ottoman Political-Economic Theory and Practice"

42. In *Nasihat üs-Selatin* to be published shortly by Andreas Tietze. I owe the reference to Professor Tietze.

43. See above, n. 38. My analysis of this important register was published as a separate monograph with the title *Bir Osmanlı Valisinin Yıllık Gelir-Gideri* (The Annual Revenues and Expenditures of an Ottoman Governor: Diyarbekir, 1670–71).

Recapitulation and Conclusion

1. *Tārih-i Naimā*, 3 : 219; *Sicill-i Osmāni*, 4 : 390.

Appendix 1

1. I used MS. TSK, EH 1515, folios 350b–383b. Both this eighteenth-century copy and the Vienna MS, published by Hadiye Tuncer (Ankara, 1964), are full of mistakes. A critical edition of this important work is long overdue.

2. Ö. L. Barkan, "Timar," pp. 290–91.

3. Ali Kemali Aksüt, *Koçi Bey Risalesi*, pp. 99–103.

4. Hamid Hadzibeǵiç, ed., "Rasprava Ali Çauşa iz Sofije o timarskoj organizaciji u XVIII stoljeço," *Bulletin du Musée de la République Populaire de Bosnie et Hercégovine à Sarajevo.*

5. Evliya Çelebi, *Seyahatnāme*, 1:182ff.

6. *Cihannümā* (Istanbul, 1145/1732) p. 411, *Sancak*s of Van province.

7. Feridun Ahmed Bey, *Münşeāt üs-Selâtin*, 2:403–7.

8. Complete disregard of Ottoman archival sources, except for such documents as have been published, seriously mars a recent study of Ottoman *sancak*s: Andreas Birken, *Die Provinzen des Osmanischen Reiches.*

9. The two *ruznāme* I have utilized in this study are BA, MAD 17893 *ruznāme* for Anadolu, covering not just Anadolu province but all of the territories in Asia Minor, for the years 892–94/1486–88; and MAD 34, Rumeli *ruznāme*, covering all of the European territories, for the years 948–49/1541–42.

10. For *sancak* lists extracted from the appointment registers, see appendixes 2–4 of the Turkish version of this study.

11. Ö. L. Barkan, "H. 933–934 (M. 1527–1528) Malî Yılına Ait Bütçe Örneği," appendix 2, pp. 303–7.

12. M. Tayyib Gökbilgin, "Kanuni Sultan Süleyman Devri Başlarında Rumeli Eyaleti, Livaları, Şehir ve Kasabaları."

13. Peçuylu İbrahim, *Tarih-i Peçūyi*, 1:84.

14. This is Güzelce Kasım Paşa, also identified by Nejat Göyünç, who gives a portion of the list in his "Diyarbekir Beylerbeyiliği'nin İdari Taksimatı," *TD* (March 1969), 23:23–34. Göyünç guesses the date of the list to be around 1526 (p. 29, n. 38).

15. *Tarih-i Peçūyi*, 1:121 and İ. H. Uzunçarşılı, *Osmanlı Tarihi*, 2:334–36.

16. *Tarih-i Peçūyi*, 1:128; also see *Sicill-i Osmânî*, 2:4.

17. *Tarih-i Peçūyi*, 1:157.

18. Nejat Göyünç, "Diyarbekir Beylerbeyiliği," p. 34.

Appendix 2

1. Cev Dah 6095 has been utilized by Şerafettin Turan, "XVII. Yüzyılda Osmanlı Imparatorluǧunun İdari Teşkilatı."

Bibliography

Unpublished Documents

Istanbul, Prime Minister's Archives (Başbakanlık Arşivi).
  Cevdet Catalogue: Cev. Dah. 6095.
  Maliyeden Müdevver Catalogue: 34, 559, 563, 4702, 17893.
  Kamil Kepeci Catalogue: 262, 266, 320, 342, 697, 717, 1865.
  Tahrīr Registers: 22, 72, 74, 107, 116, 118, 119, 125, 135, 141, 227, 231, 269.
Istanbul, Topkapı Palace Archives.
  Registers: D.5246, D.8303, D.10057.

Published Documents and Studies on Documents

Anhegger, Robert and Halil İnalcık, eds. *Kānūnnāme-i Sultānī ber mūceb-i Örf-i Osmānī*. Ankara, 1956.

Barkan, Ömer Lütfi. *XV ve XVI'ıncı Asırlarda Osmanlı İmparatorluğunda Zirāi Ekonominin Hukukī ve Mālī Esasları*, Vol. 1: *Kanunlar*. Istanbul, 1943.

Barkan, Ömer Lütfi. "H. 933–934 (M. 1527–1528) Māli Yılına Ait Bütçe Örneği." *İFM* (1953–54), 15:251–329.

Barkan, Ömer Lütfi. "Edirne Askeri Kassamına Ait Tereke Defterleri, 1545–1659." *Belgeler* (1966), 3:1–479.

Barkan, Ömer Lütfi and Ekrem Hakkı Ayverdi. *İstanbul Vakıfları Tahrir Defteri*. Istanbul, 1970.

Beldiceanu, Nicoara, ed. *Les Actes des Premiers Sultans, I: Actes de Mehmed II et de Bayezid II du MS. Fonds Turc Ancien 39*. Paris and The Hague, 1960.

Beldiceanu, Nicoara, ed. *Les Actes des Premiers Sultans, II: Règlements Miniers, 1390–1512*. Paris and The Hague, 1964.

Beldiceanu-Steinherr, Irene. *Recherches sur les actes des règnes des sultans Osman, Orkhan et Murad I*. Munich, 1967.

Fekete, Lajos. *Die Siyaqat-Schrift in der Turkischen Finanzverwaltung*. 2 vols. Budapest, 1955.

Feridun Ahmed Bey. *Münşeāt üs-Selātīn.* 2 vols. Istanbul, 1247.

Gökbilgin, Tayyib. *XV–XVI. Asırlarda Edirne ve Paşa Livası.* Istanbul, 1952.

Gökbilgin, Tayyib. "Kanuni Sultan Süleyman Devri Başlarında Rumeli Eyaleti, Livaları, Şehir ve Kasabaları." *Belleten* (1964), 20:247–294.

Gökbilgin, Tayyib. "Venedik Devlet Arşivindeki Vesikalar Külliyatında Kanuni Sultan Süleyman Devri Belgeleri." *Belgeler* (1964), 1:119–220.

Gökbilgin, Tayyib. "Kanuni Sultan Süleyman'in Timar ve Zeamet Tevcihi ile İlgili Fermanları." *TD* (1967), 17:35–48.

Gökbilgin, Tayyib. "Venedik Devlet Arşivindeki Türkçe Belgeler Koleksiyonu ve Bizimle İlgili Diğer Belgeler." *Belgeler* (1971), 7–8:1–151.

Heyd, Uriel. *Studies in Old Ottoman Criminal Law.* V. L. Ménage, ed. Oxford, 1973.

İnalcık, Halil. "Adaletnāmeler." *Belgeler* (1965), 2:49–145.

İnalcık, Halil, ed., *Sūret-i Defter-i Sancak-ı Arvānid.* Ankara, 1954.

Lugal, Necati and Adnan Erzi, eds. *Fatih Devrine Ait Münşeāt Mecmuası.* Istanbul, 1956.

Mehmed Arif, ed. *Kānūnnāme-i Āl-i Osmān.* Istanbul, 1330.

Orhonlu, Cengiz. *Telhisler.* Istanbul, 1970.

Özkaya, Yücel. "XVIII'inci Yüzyılda Çıkarılan Adalet-nāmelere Göre Türkiye'nin İç Durumu." *Belleten* (1974), 38:445–491.

Sahillioğlu, Halil. "Osmanlı İdaresinde Kıbrıs'ın İlk Yılı Bütçesi." *Belgeler* (1967), 4:1–33.

Shaw, Stanford J. *The Budget of Ottoman Egypt, 1005–1006.* The Hague and Paris, 1968.

Turan, Şerafettin. "XVII. Yüzyılda Osmanlı İmparatorluğunun İdari Taksimatı." *Atatürk Üniversitesi Yıllığı. 1961,* pp. 201–232.

Works By Contemporary Ottoman Writers

Āli, Mustafa. *Mevāid ün-Nefāis fi Kavā'id ül-Mecālis.* Istanbul, 1956.

Aşıkpaşazāde Tarihi. Ali Bey, ed. Istanbul, 1332.

Anhegger, Robert. "Hezarfen Hüseyin Efendi'nin Osmanlı Devlet Teşkilatına Dair Mūlahazaları." *Türkiyat Mecmuası* (1951–53), 10:365–393.

Ayni Ali Makalesi. Topkapı Palace Library. MS. EH. 1515, ff. 350b–383b.

Dukanovic, Marija, ed. *Rimovana Autobiografija Varvari Ali-Paşe.* Belgrad, 1967.

Evliya Çelebi. *Seyahatname.* Istanbul, 1314–1938.

Hadzibeǵic, Hamid, ed. "Rasprava Ali Çauşa iz Sofije o timarskoj organizaciji u XVII stoljecu." *Bulletin du Musée de la République Populaire de Bosnia et Hercégovine à Sarajevo* (1947), N. S. 2:139–206.

Hasan el-Kāfi el-Akhisāri. *Usūl el-Hikem fi Nizām ül-Ālem.* Istanbul, 1295.

Katip Çelebi. *Balance of Truth.* G. L. Lewis, trans. London, 1963.

Katip Çelebi. *Cihannümā.* Istanbul, 1145.

Katip Çelebi. *Düstūr el-Amel li-İslāh el-Halel.* Istanbul, 1280.

Koçi Bey Risalesi. Ali Kemali Aksüt, ed. Istanbul, 1939.
Lütfi Paşa. *Asâfnâme.* Rudolf Tschudi, ed. and trans. Berlin, 1910.
Naimâ, Mustafa. *Târih-i Naimâ.* Istanbul, 1280.
Peçuylu İbrahim, *Târih-i Peçüyi.* Istanbul 1281–1283.
Selâniki, Mustafa. *Târih-i Selâniki.* Istanbul, 1281.
Tuncer, Hadiye, ed. *Osmanlı Imparatorluğunda Eyalet Taksimatı, Toprak Dağıtımı ve Bunların Mali Güçleri.* Ankara, 1964.
Yücel, Yaşar, ed. *Kitâb-ı Müstetâb.* Ankara, 1974.

Modern Studies

Abou-el-Haj, Rifaat Ali. "The Ottoman Vezir and Paşa Households, 1683–1703: A Preliminary Report." *JAOS* (1974), 94:438–447.
Akdağ, Mustafa. *Türkiye'nin İktisadi ve İçtimai Tarihi.* 2 vols. Ankara, 1959 and 1971.
Akdağ, Mustafa. *Celâli İsyanları.* Ankara, 1963.
Akdağ, Mustafa. "Osmanlı Imparatorluğunun Yükselişi Devrinde Esas Düzen." *TAD* (1965), 3:139–156.
Akdağ, Mustafa. "Genel Çizgileriyle XVII. Yüzyıl Türkiye Tarihi." *TAD* (1966), 4:201–247.
Ayalon, David. *L'Esclavage du Mamelouk.* Jerusalem, 1951.
Ayalon, David. *Gunpowder and Firearms in the Mamluk Kingdom.* London, 1956.
Ayalon, David. "Studies in al-Jabarti." *JESHO* (1970), 13:195–211.
Ayalon, David. "Aspects of the Mamluk Phenomenon." *Der Islam* (1976), 53:196–225.
Barkan, Ömer Lütfi. "Osmanlı İmaratorluğunun Bütçelerine Dair Notlar." *İFM* (1953–1954), 15:238–250.
Barkan, Ömer Lüfti. "XVI. Yüzyılın İkinci Yarısında Türkiye'de Fiat Hareketleri." *Belleten* (1970), 34:557–607.
Barkan, Ömer Lütfi. "Timar." *İA.*
Barkan Ömer Lütfi. "The Price Revolution of the Sixteenth Century: A Turning Point in the Economic History of the Near East." *IJMES* (1975), 6:3–28.
Berkes, Niyazi. *Yüz Soruda Türkiye İktisat Tarihi.* 2 vols. Istanbul 1969 and 1970.
Birken, Andreas. *Die Provinzen des Osmanischen Reiches.* Wiesbanden, 1976.
Bulliet, Richard W. "A Quantitative Approach to Medieval Muslim Biographical Dictionaries." *JESHO* (1973), 4:195–211.
Cezar, Mustafa. *Osmanlı Tarihinde Leventler.* Istanbul, 1965.
Cohen, Amnon and Bernard Lewis. *Population and Revenue in the Towns of Palestine in the Sixteenth Century.* Princeton, 1978.
Cook. M. A. *Population Pressure in Rural Anatolia.* London, 1972.
Danişmend, İsmail Hami. *İzahlı Osmanlı Tarihi Kronolojisi.* 4 vols. Istanbul 1951.
Deny, J. "Sancak," *IA.*

Faroqhi, Suraiya. "Social Mobility and the Ottoman Ulema in the Later Sixteenth Century." *IJMES* (1973), 4:204–218.
Faroqhi, Suraiya. "Rural Society in Anatolia and the Balkans during the Sixteenth Century," part I. *Turcica* (1977), 9(1):161–196.
Filipoviç, Nedim. "Bosna-Hersek'te Timar Sisteminin İnkişafında Bazı Hususiyetler." *İFM* (1953–1954), 15:155–188.
Forand, Paul G. "The Relation of the Slave and the Client to the Master or Patron." *IJMES* (1971), 2:59–66.
Genç, Mehmed. "Osmanlı Maliyesinde Mālikāne Sistemi." In Osman Okyar, ed., *Türkiye İktisat Tarihi Semineri.* Ankara, 1975.
Gerber, Haim. "Seventeenth-Century Anatolian City of Bursa," Ph.D. diss., Hebrew University, 1976.
Gibb, H. A. R. "Tarikh." *Encyclopedia of Islam, Supplement.*
Gibb, H. A. R. and Harold Bowen. *Islamic Society and the West.* Vol. 1, parts 1 and 2. Oxford, 1950, 1957.
Gökbilgin, Tayyib. "XVI. Asır Başlarında Kayseri Şehri ve Livası." In *Zeki Velidi Togan'a Armağan,* pp. 93–108. Istanbul, 1950–55.
Gökbilgin, Tayyib. "Yeni Belgelerin Işığı Altında Kanuni Sultan Süleyman Devrinde Osmanlı-Venedik Münasebetleri." *Kanuni Armağanı,* pp. 171–186. Ankara, 1970.
Gökbilgin, Tayyib. "Müteferrika." *İA.*
Göyünç, Nejat. "Diyarbekir Beylerbeyiliği'nin İlk İdari Taksimatı." *TD* (1969), 23:23–34.
Holt, P. M. *Egypt and the Fertile Crescent.* London, 1966.
Holt, P. M. "The Pattern of Egyptian Political History from 1517 to 1798." In P.M. Holt, ed., *Political and Social Change in Modern Egypt.* London, 1968.
İnalcık, Halil. "Ottoman Methods of Conquest." *Studia Islamica* (1954), 2:103–129.
İnalcık, Halil. "Osmanlılarda Raiyyet Rüsūmu." *Belleten* (1959), 23:575–610.
İnalcık, Halil, "Balaban," "Çiftlik," "Djizya—Ottoman Empire," "Eyālet," "Ghulām—Ottoman Empire," *EI* (2).
İnalcık, Halil. "Capital Formation in the Ottoman Empire." *Journal of Economic History* (1969), 29:97–140.
İnalcık, Halil. "The Emergence of the Ottomans," "The Rise of the Ottoman Empire," "The Heyday and Decline of the Ottoman Empire." In P. M. Holt, Ann K. S. Lambton, and Bernard Lewis, eds., *The Cambridge History of Islam,* 1:263–353. Cambridge, 1970.
İnalcık, Halil. *The Ottoman Empire: The Classical Age, 1300–1600.* London, 1973.
İnalcık, Halil. "Centralization and Decentralization in Ottoman Administration." T. Naff and R. Owen, eds., *Studies in Eighteenth Century Islamic History,* pp. 27–52. (Carbondale Southern Illinois University Press 1977).
Itzkowitz, Norman. "Eighteenth-Century Ottoman Realities." *Studia Islamica* (1962), 16:73–94.
Itzkowitz, Norman. *Islamic Tradition and the Ottoman Empire.* New York, 1972.

Itzkowitz, Norman and Joel Shinder. "The Office of Şeyh ül-Islām and the Tanzimat—A Prosopographic Enquiry." *Middle Eastern Studies* (1972), 8: 94–101.

Köprülü, Fuad. *Les Origines de l'Empire Ottoman.* Paris, 1935. Enlarged Turkish translation, *Osmanlı Devletinin Kuruluşu.* Ankara, 1959.

Kunt, İ. Metin. "The Köprülü Years: 1656–1661." Ph.D. diss., Princeton University, 1971.

Kunt, İ. Metin. "Ethnic-Regional (*Cins*) Solidarity in the Seventeenth-Century Ottoman Establishment." *IJMES* (1974), 5: 233–239.

Kunt, İ. Metin. "Kulların Kulları." *Boğaziçi Üniversitesi Dergisi—Hümaniter Bilimler* (1975), 3: 27–42.

Kunt, İ. Metin. "Derviş Mehmed Paşa, Vezir and Entrepreneur: A Study in Ottoman Political-Economic Theory and Practice." *Turcica* (1977), 9(1): 197–214.

Kunt, İ. Metin, *Bir Osmanlı Valisinin Yıllık Gelir-Gideri, Diyarbekir 1670–71* Istanbul, 1981.

Kütükoğlu, Bekir, *Osmanlı-İran Siyasi Münasebetleri* Istanbul, 1962.

Lewis, Bernard. "Ottoman Observers of Ottoman Decline." *Islamic Studies* (1962), 1: 71–87.

Lindner, Rudi Paul. "Ottoman Government and Nomad Society." Ph.D. diss., University of California, Berkeley, 1976.

Lybyer, Albert H. *The Government of the Ottoman Empire in the Time of Suleiman the Magnificent.* Cambridge, Mass., 1913.

Mantran, Robert. *Istanbul dans la Seconde Moitié de 17e Siècle.* Paris 1962.

McGowan, Bruce. "Food Supply and Taxation on the Middle Danube (1568–1579)." *Archivum Ottomanicum* (1969), 1: 138–196.

Ménage, V. L. "Beglerbeg," "Devshirme," *EI* (2).

Ménage, V. L. "Some Notes on the *Devshirme*," *BSOAS* (1966), 29: 64–78.

Miller, Barnette. *The Palace School of Mohammad the Conqueror.* Cambridge, Mass., 1941.

Mustafa Nuri Paşa. *Netāic ül-Vukūāt.* 3 vols. Istanbul, 1327.

Papoulia, Basilike D. *Ursprung und Wesen der Knabenlese im Osmanischen Reich.* Munich, 1963.

Pitcher, Donald Edgar. *An Historical Geography of the Ottoman Empire.* Leiden, 1972.

Rosenthal, Franz, *A History of Muslim Historiography.* Leiden, 1968.

Shaw, Standford J. "The Ottoman View of the Balkans." In C. Jelavich and B. Jelavich, eds., *The Balkans in Transition.* Berkeley and Los Angeles, 1963.

Shaw, Stanford J. *The Financial and Administrative Organization and Development of Ottoman Egypt, 1517–1798.* Princeton, 1962.

Shinder, Joel. "Early Ottoman Administration in the Wilderness: Some Limits on Comparison," *IJMES* (1978), 9: 497–517.

Shmuelevitz, Aryeh. "Capsali as a Source for Ottoman History, 1450–1523." *IJMES* (1978), 9: 339–344.

Stone, Lawrence. "Prosopography." *Daedalus* (Winter 1971), pp. 46–79.

Süreyya, Mehmed. *Sicill-i Osmāni.* Istanbul, 1308–1311.

Uğur, Ali. "The Ottoman Ulemā in the Mid-seventeenth Century: An Analysis of the *Vakāʿiʿül-Fuzalā* of Mehmed Şeyhi Efendi." Ph.D. diss. Edinburgh University, 1973.

Uzunçarşılı, İsmail Hakkı. *Kapıkulu Ocakları.* 2 vols. Ankara 1943 and 1944.

Uzunçarşılı, İsmail Hakkı. *Osmanlı Tarihi,* Vols. I–III Ankara, 1947–1954.

Wittek, Paul. *The Rise of the Ottoman Empire.* London, 1938.

Wittek, Paul. "De la Defaite d'Ankara a la Prise de Constantinople." *Revue des Etudes Islamiques* (1938), 12:1–34.

Wittek, Paul. "*Devshirme* and *Shariʿa.*" *BSOAS* (1955), 17:271–278.

Yücel, Yaşar. "Osmanlı İmparatorluğunda Desantralizasyona Dair Genel Gözlemler." *Belleten* (1974), 38:657–708.

Index

87–88, 90, 95–96, 98
Defterdār (secretary of finance), 6
Defterdār-ı māl (provincial financial officer)
    28, 92; *see also Hazine defterdārı*
Delhi, 7
Devşirme (non-Muslim recruits), 7, 9, 45;
    defined, 32; abandoned, 76, 97
Dirlik system: emergence, 4; defined, 9;
    rationale, 15, 22, 85–87; *see also* Decline
    of the *dirlik* system
Dismissal of *dirlik* holders, 24–25
Divān (beylerbeyi's council), 28
Divān-ı humāyūn, 6; *see also* Imperial council
Diyarbekir province, 91–93, 158n5
Dizdār (fortress commander), 22
Duke of Savoy, 41
Dulkadir state, 39
Dulkadriye province, *see* Maraş province

Edirne, 5–6, 86, 89
Eger, *see* Eğri province
Eğri province, 90, 134
Egypt, xiii, 32, 39, 79; province, 91, 158n5
Ehl-i ilm (men of knowledge), xiv; *see also*
    Ulemā
Ehl-i kalem (men of the pen), xiv
Ehl-i seyf (men of the sword), xiv
Emirahur (head of imperial stables), 6
Emiralem (chief of imperial band and
    tentsetters), 6
Emirate, xx; *see also Beylik* (principality)
Enderūn (palace school, inner service),
    xix–xx, 6–7, 39, 46, 65–67, 96–97; *see
    also* Pages in palace; Palace
Erzurum province, 15, 49–50, 63, 90, 134
Estates, *see Ümerā*
Estate of Yunus Bey, 48
Europe, 3, 41, 78, 99; *see also* Western
    transformation; Western military
    challenge
Europeans, 7, 31–33
Evliya Çelebi, official and traveller, xx,
    96–97, 102

Faroqhi, S., xvii
Ferman, 12, 40
Ferhad Paşa, a vezir, 85
Filek *sancak*, abolished, 90

Financial bureaucracy, 5
Fines, 9, 52; *see also Cürm ve cināyet*
Firearms, 164n5
France, 31
Frontier: conditions, 79, 84; families, 56;
    region, 4, 40, 163n40; *sancak*s, 23, 49, 63,
    71; Selçuklu-Byzantine, 1–2
Frontiersmen, 2–5, 35; *see also Akıncı; Ghāzi*

Genoese, 41
Gerber, H., 52
Ghāzi, 35; *see also Akıncı*; Frontiersmen
Gökbilgin, T., 103
Golden age, xv
Göyünç, N., 167n14
Grand vezir, xiv, xviii, 6, 32, 35, 41, 50,
    96, 117–8
Granting of *dirlik*s regulated, 38
Great Selçuklus, 5
Greece, 20
Group biography, xvi, xxi; *see also*
    Prosopography
Gulām (slave), 41, 44, 163n23; *see also Kul*;
    Slaves

Hadīkat ül-Vüzerā, xviii
Hadith (sayings of Muhammad), xviii
Halep (Aleppo), *sancak* 20; province 49,
    63, 134
Hamīlet ül-Kübera, xviii
Hapsburg Empire, 78–79, 138; *see also*
    Austrian campaign; Austrian front;
    Austrians; Austrian turncoat
Harem, 47
Hās: defined, 12–13; levels, 27, 50–51,
    83–84
Hasan el-Kāfi el-Akhisāri, a kādı and
    author, 79
Hasan Paşa, Abaza, 93
Hasan Paşa, Yemişçi, a grand vezir, 84
Havāss-ı humāyūn (imperial reserves), 13,
    20; *see also* Sultan's income
Hazine defterdārı, defined, 28; 119; *see also*
    Defterdār-ı māl (provincial financial
    officer)
Hersek *sancak*, 40, 158n1
Herzegovina, *see* Hersek *sancak*
Heyd, U., 52